WITHDRAWN

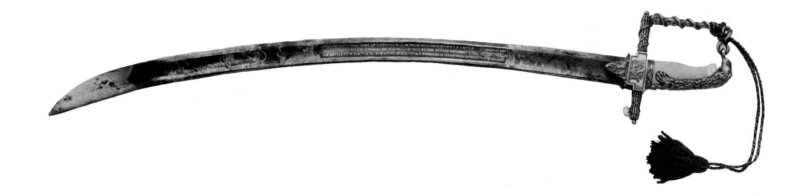

Antique Weapons A–Z

DOUGLAS J. FRYER

THOMAS NELSON INC.

New York   Camden

All rights reserved under International and Pan-American Conventions.
Published by Thomas Nelson Inc., Camden, New Jersey.

First U.S. edition

Library of Congress Catalog Card Number: 70-160145
International Standard Book Number: 0-8407-4319-X

Originally published by G. Bell & Sons Ltd, London

Manufactured in Great Britain

Contents

Acknowledgements

All photographic illustrations are of items that have passed through the salerooms of Messrs Wallis & Wallis of Lewes, with the exception of the following, which are from the author's collection: 28–35, 109, 138–9, 216–28, 300–5, and of 15, which is from the P. Bedford Collection.

Firearms & Accessories

Adams   Robert Adams, a London gunsmith, patented a self-cocking percussion revolver in 1851, as a challenge to Colonel Samuel Colt's single-action revolver. Three models were produced in 38, 54 and 120 bore (75). The double-action Beaumont-Adams revolver followed in 1855 (46). Other models followed subsequently on the breech-loading system (81).

Afghan Butt   A distinctive form of stock found on guns from Sind. The butt has a pronounced curve behind the lock and then sweeps into a wide end, its shape appearing to be almost triangular (178).

Air Cane   A type of pump-up air gun made in the form of a walking stick. The air reservoir was contained in the detachable butt. Some had an alternative rifled barrel which was inserted into the smooth-bore barrel (12).

Air Gun   A form of weapon first introduced in the late sixteenth century. Some had the air reservoir contained in the butt or in a tube around the barrel, others had a spherical reservoir which was mounted in front of the trigger-guard (173). Another variety had a bellows pump in the butt, operated by a crank lever (179). Early air guns had a complete dummy flintlock action, the cock acting as the cocking lever. This was intended to disguise the fact that they were air weapons because these were, for a time, illegal.

Air Pistol   Hand weapons of this type were made with similar actions to the air guns. Early air pistols are much rarer than the long guns (36).

Alarm Gun   There were two uses for Alarm Guns: (1) To warn of poachers or intruders. A gun designed for this purpose had a barrel containing a charge and was operated by a trip wire or by opening a door. (2) To annouce the time of day. This type was in the form of a sundial mounted with a small cannon barrel, the charge of which was ignited by the rays of the sun concentrated through a lens.

Allen   Numerous models of American percussion pocket pistols and pepperboxes, percussion and early cartridge revolvers were produced by E. Allen & Co. of Grafton, Mass., Allen & Thurber and Allen & Wheelock of Worcester, Mass. (103).

Apache Pistol   The term given to a combination weapon, usually a revolver with folding dagger blade and knuckleduster grip. The name is derived from their use by the 'Apache' thugs of Paris (155).

Arquebus   A light form of hand gun of the sixteenth and early seventeenth centuries. Some had the butt curved for firing from the chest rather than the shoulder.

Axe-pistol   A combination weapon, being a pistol with axe blade attached. European wheel-lock and flintlock specimens are known, also Indian examples with matchlock ignition (108, 109).

Back-action   A type of lock mechanism with the mainspring set behind the hammer.

Back-sight   The grooved sight at the breech end of a firearm barrel, which was aligned with the foresight. Some had two or more folding leaves of different elevation in order to vary the range of the weapon.

Back Strap   The strip or band of metal along the back of a pistol or revolver grip.

Baker Percussion Revolver   In 1852 T. K. Baker patented a transition-type (*q.v.*) percussion revolver. It was a single-action weapon with an extended hammer spur for easy cocking.

Baker Rifle   A military flintlock rifle designed by Ezekiel Baker, a London gunsmith, and used in the British Service from about 1800 to 1838.

Ball Butt   A spherical form of butt found on some wheel-lock pistols, Cossack pistols, etc. (*19, 20*).

Ball Trigger   A trigger in the form of a ball, usually without a guard. It is found on Scottish pistols, Caucasian firearms, and elsewhere (*15, 19*).

Baltic Lock   A type of lock introduced in the middle of the sixteenth century and similar in form to the Scandinavian snap lock. It had a long curved cock and a frizzen, or steel, which hinged out sideways (*214*).

Baluster Turn   A turned band or 'step' found on a pistol or gun barrel. Usually found on seventeenth- and eighteenth-century pieces.

Bandolier   A cross belt, worn over the shoulder and used for carrying cartridges. Early types had the chargers suspended from them and those of recent date have loops to take the cartridges.

Barrel Key   A type of spanner used to unscrew the screw-barrel usually found on pocket pistols. Two types are found: (1) A ring which fits on the outside of the barrel over the lug provided and (2) the plug variety which engages in notches inside the muzzle. Either type is often to be found combined with a nipple key.

Barrel Loop   A small loop (or loops) beneath a pistol or gun barrel, through which a pin is passed to secure it to the stock.

Barrel Step   See *Baluster Turn*.

Bell Muzzle   A swelling out of the muzzle in the shape of a bell, in order to spread the shot (*139, 170, 171*).

Belted Ball   A type of bullet with a raised band around it, which was used in the rifle with two deep grooves of rifling, an example being the Brunswick Rifle (*q.v.*).

Belt Hook   A long steel clip, sometimes ornamental, fitted to the side of a pistol for the purpose of carrying it on the belt or sash.

Belt Pistol   A pistol fitted with a belt hook (*q.v.*). The term is generally used to refer to a medium-length pistol of the mid-nineteenth century. Pistols of varying length and age are found fitted with belt hooks and it is a characteristic feature of the Scottish all-metal pistol.

Bent   The notches in the underside of the tumbler (*q.v.*) in which the sear engages at the half-cock and full-cock positions. Irish-made pistols frequently have three bents to the action. See *Flintlock*.

Bird's-head Butt   A self-descriptive term, being a pistol or revolver with the butt similar in shape to the head of a bird. Some French pistols had this form of butt; also some American pistols and revolvers, and some Webley cartridge-loading revolvers.

Blueing   A form of artificial rusting, which is applied to the steel parts of a firearm to produce a coloured finish of varying hues from blue to black. It protects the metal against rust and prevents the reflection of light on the barrel in use.

Blunderbuss   A short form of musket with a barrel widening at the muzzle in order to scatter the shot. Many were made with brass barrels and some were fitted with a spring-bayonet. Blunderbusses were used for home defence, in mail coaches and by the services (*170, 171, 176, 199*). See also *Bell Muzzle*.

Blunderbuss Pistol   A pistol fitted with a blunderbuss-type barrel generally of large bore with a flared or bell-mouth muzzle (*2, 28, 139*).

Bolton Lock   A patent screwless flintlock with the mechanism enclosed between two steel plates. It was the invention of George Bolton and was made by Henry Nock.

Bootleg Pistol   A percussion boxlock pistol with underhammer action and no trigger guard. The butt is often of the 'saw-handle' type (*q.v.*).

Bore   The interior of the barrel of a firearm. This term is also used to indicate the calibre of the weapon: i.e. 'twelve bore' means that the size of the bore will take a ball, twelve of which would weigh 1 lb.

Bore Gauge   A tapered plug which is inserted in the muzzle of a firearm to determine its bore size. The gauge bears a graduated scale for this purpose.

Bow Gun or Catapult Gun   A longarm in which the projectile was fired by catapult elastic. The 'barrel' was open both sides and some models had a small bow at the muzzle end. A maker's name often encountered is Hodges, who was granted a patent in 1849.

Boxlock   A type of pistol or gun action in which the mechanism is contained within the frame (*3–6, 28–31, 34, 35*).

Breech   The rear portion of the barrel of a firearm wherein the charge is contained.

Breech-loading   A firearm which is loaded at the breech end.

Breech Plug   A removable screw-in plug in the breech end of the barrel of a muzzle-loading firearm.

Bridle   A small plate in the lock of a firearm which provides additional strength. It caps the tumbler and is secured by the sear screw. See *Flintlock*.

Brown Bess   The familiar name given to the British standard military flintlock musket used in varying forms during the eighteenth century and the first half of the nineteenth century. The earlier types had barrels of 46 inches then 42 inches in length from about 1740 and about 1800 the standard length became 39 inches, the latter known as the 'India Pattern'. They were equipped with a triangular-bladed socket bayonet (*195*).

Browning   A brown finish similar to blueing (*q.v.*), which when applied to a twist barrel heightens the fine pattern.

Brunswick Rifle   The British service percussion longarm adopted about 1838. The rifling was its distinctive feature, having only two deep semicircular grooves. The bullet used with this weapon was the belted ball (*q.v.*).

Bullet Mould   An implement, usually of pincer form, with cavity or cavities into which molten lead is poured to cast bullets. A sprue cutter is often fitted to the bullet mould. The sprue is the small lug of lead remaining attached to the cast bullet and formed at the mouth of the cavity. Good-quality double or single cavity brass moulds were included with cased English percussion revolvers. Bullet moulds often bear the initials W.D. This refers to the maker William Davis and is not a War Department mark, as is often thought (*224, 228*). See also *Gang Mould*.

Butt   The rear end of the stock of a firearm.

Butt Cap   A metal mount which was affixed to the end of a pistol butt. It was frequently ornamental, made of brass, gilt metal or silver, sometimes in the form of a grotesque mask.

Butt Plate   The metal plate used to cover and protect the heel of a gun butt. It is usually engraved *en suite* with the other mounts.

Butt-trap   A compartment in the butt of a firearm used to contain cleaning implements, spare parts, percussion caps, etc. Those on pistols have spring-back covers often forming part of the butt cap.

Calibre   The diameter of the bore measured across the lands (*q.v.*). In Britain and America it is noted in inches and on the continent of Europe in millimetres.

Caliver   A light form of early hand gun, usually with matchlock ignition.

Cane Gun   A walking stick containing a gun. Examples are seen with flintlock, percussion and cartridge systems. Some are air guns, and these are usually all steel and often have an alternative rifled barrel. Cane guns were used for self-defence, by poachers and sportsmen (*12*).

Cannon-barrel   A form of pistol barrel similar to that of a cannon, slightly tapering towards the muzzle, which has a raised band. Usually seen on late-seventeenth-century and eighteenth-century pistols. Often referred to as Queen Anne type (*33, 128, 134*).

Cannon Igniter   A device, often fitted with a flint or percussion lock, used to ignite the flash powder on a cannon (*110*).

Cap Dispenser   A container, usually of brass, to hold a quantity of percussion caps and made to release one cap at a time when placed on the nipple. The caps are spring-loaded in the dispenser. Two types are found: (1) circular and (2) straight-bar. See example in cased *Paterson Colt*.

Capping Breech Loader   A late percussion-ignition firearm in which a combustible cartridge was loaded at the breech end. Well-known examples are the Westley Richards 'monkey tail', Terry's patent, Prince's patent and Greene's patent (*183*).

Cap Tin   A small japanned container for percussion caps, often found in cased sets. The maker's label is generally found on the lid of the tin (*221*).

Carbine   A short rifle, or musket, often used as a cavalry weapon.

Carbine Butt   A detachable butt-stock fitted to a holster pistol to enable it to be used as a carbine (*50*).

Cartouche   A pouch to contain cartridges, worn on the belt.

Cartridge   The charge for a firearm, usually combining the propellent explosive and the bullet. Later types, i.e. pinfire, rimfire and centre fire, also contained the detonating device.

Cartridge Display   A manufacturer's display advertisement shown in retail shops. Various types of military and sporting ammunition were attractively mounted in a glass-fronted case, together with specimens of wads, caps, shot and other items (*244*).

Cased Pistols   Pairs of pistols, revolvers, etc., were frequently sold in an oak or mahogany case. These were lined with velvet or baize and had compartments containing accessories (*1–14, 47–55*).

Centre-fire   A cartridge in which the detonator is in the centre of the base of the case.

Chamber   The part of the barrel, at the breech end, which contains the charge. In a revolver the chambers are, of course, the cylinder.

Chequering   A 'criss-cross' hatching of the stock of a firearm in order that a better grip be obtained when in use. Sometimes an ornamental design was incorporated.

Cock   The movable arm on a firearm lock, which holds the flint or pyrites, the action of which against the steel (frizzen) creates a spark to ignite the charge. See *Flintlock*.

Collier   Elisha Collier of Boston, Massachusetts, came to England in 1818 and patented a flintlock revolver. This was a most advanced weapon for its time and is considered to be the first practical type of revolver to have been produced. Both revolving pistols and longarms were produced and a special feature was the automatic priming magazine that was fitted to the frizzen (*40, 204*).

Colt   Samuel Colt, born in 1814, was famous for his patent revolvers. Numerous models were developed and produced over the years, commencing with the Paterson in 1836. Three sizes of these were made, described as Pocket Pistol, Belt Pistol and Holster Pistol with calibres ranging between ·28 and ·36. Revolving rifles and shot guns were also made. The distinctive feature of the pistols was the folding trigger and lack of trigger guard. The barrels usually bore the marking *Patent Arms M'g Co. Paterson N.J. Colt's Patent*. All Paterson Colts are rare and valuable (*49*). The next production was the Army revolver Model 1847, calibre ·44, six shot, made at Whitneyville, Conn., known as the 'Walker Colt'. It was a large pistol weighing 4 lb, and is also extremely rare and valuable. Various percussion models followed, made at Hartford, Conn., including the ·44 Dragoons, ·36 Navy 1851 (octagonal barrel), ·31 Pockets (model 1849, etc.), ·44 Army 1860, ·36 Navy 1861 (round barrel), ·36 Police 1862, Roots Patent 1855 sidehammer, etc. Many of these were cased with accessories and some superb presentation engraved specimens were produced (*47, 48, 50–2, 58, 59, 61–4, 67–72*). As metallic cartridges were introduced some of the percussion Colt revolvers were converted to the breech-loading system. The famous single-action Army and Frontier, or Peacemaker, was developed from these (*60, 65, 80*). The company then went on to produce many models of single-shot ·41 Derringer pistols, rimfire and centre-fire revolvers and automatics (*13, 91, 168, 169*).

Combination Tool   A multi-purpose tool for use with a firearm. In the wheel-lock era it might consist of a spanner for cocking the weapon, a turnscrew, a powder measure, a hammer, etc. Later types combined a nipple key with pricker, oil bottle, worm and turnscrew.

Combination Weapons   A firearm combined with another weapon, e.g. knife-pistol (*q.v.*), axe-pistol, sword-pistol, or polearm with pistol (*24–6, 108, 109, 158*).

Concealed Trigger   A type of folding trigger which fits flush into the frame of a pistol when not in use. It springs out when the weapon is cocked. Also known as a hidden trigger.

Conversion   A firearm in which the means of ignition has been altered from the form in which it was originally made. Most conversions were from flintlock to percussion. As the latter system came more into use, owners of flintlock weapons had theirs converted. This was effected by the replacement of the cock with a percussion hammer, and the removal of the frizzen. The latter was then replaced by a nipple, either set in a completely new breech, or in a drum plug which was screwed into the barrel at the touch hole. The last method was, of course, a cheaper one.

Cookson   John Cookson was a well-known English late seventeenth-century maker of repeating flintlock firearms on the Lorenzoni principle. This system had magazines in the butt for powder and ball. The lock was fitted with a small magazine for priming powder. By holding the weapon in certain positions and by use of a side-lever, the weapon was primed and charged (*42*).

Curiosa   'Firearms Curiosa' is a term applied to many varieties of strange and odd weapons, e.g. combination pieces, knife pistols, cane guns, palm pistols, knuckleduster pistols, and alarm and trap guns (*24–6, 108–11, 155–8, 160, 161*).

Cylinder   The revolving chambered breech of a firearm. Most cylinders are five or six shot but a few were made to take twelve or even more cartridges. The action of the weapon usually rotates the cylinder but on some early revolvers it had to be rotated by hand.

Dag   A small pistol, usually wheel-lock, of the late sixteenth and early seventeenth centuries. It was a short clumsy weapon with ball butt.

Damascening   A form of decoration on weapons where gold or silver is hammered onto the metal surface.

Damascus Barrel   A barrel formed from thin bars of iron and steel intricately twisted and welded together. The result is an attractive pattern, which is sometimes heightened by etching or browning.

Deringer   A small compact single-shot pistol usually of large bore. The name is derived from a percussion pistol of this type produced by Henry Deringer of Philadelphia in the mid-nineteenth century (*159, 168, 169*).

Detent   A lever acting as a check in the tumbler mechanism of a firearm lock, to prevent the sear from engaging accidentally on the half-cock bent.

Dog Lock   An early form of flintlock action where a hooked catch engages on the heel of the cock to serve as a safety device.

Double Action   A type of revolver mechanism in which the act of pulling the trigger cocks the hammer, rotates the cylinder and fires the weapon (77).

Double-barrelled   As the term implies, a firearm with two barrels. These may be side-by-side or over-and-under (superimposed) (*29, 39, 120, 123, 124*).

Double-trigger   A revolver action, as on a Tranter (*q.v.*), where there are two triggers, one above the other. The lower trigger cocks the weapon and the upper trigger fires it (*55*).

Drum Conversion   A cheap form of conversion from flintlock to percussion system, where a drum-shaped plug, fitted with a nipple, is screwed into the barrel in place of the touch hole.

Duck-gun   A long gun of large bore used for wild fowling. The barrel was usually about 6 feet in length.

Duck's Foot   Also known as a *Mob Pistol*, this weapon has four barrels, usually splayed out, to discharge a volley of bullets simultaneously. They are thought to have been used by sea captains when faced with a mutinous crew (*157*).

Duelling Pistol   A type of pistol evolved in England about 1770. It was about 16 to 18 inches in length with a barrel of approximately 10 inches, having a fairly small bore. The early examples were full-stocked and somewhat plain in design. Around the turn of the century the barrels were octagonal in form and the pistols frequently half-stocked. Many had the quality features of gold or platinum touch-holes and gold-lined pans, set-trigger mechanisms and patent breeching. As the system of ignition changed from flintlock, duelling pistols were made on the new principles of detonator, pellet lock, tube lock and finally percussion. The mounts were of finely engraved and blued steel, or silver on the high-quality weapons. Some were fitted with the 'saw-handle' butt (*q.v.*). Duelling Pistols were made in pairs and cased sets are frequently encountered, complete with accessories. The latter comprised bullet mould, powder flask (often with base trap for flints or caps, and ball compartment), patches, loading/cleaning rod and mallet, turnscrew, spare flints or tin of percussion caps, etc. Some well-known makers were Griffin & Tow, Wogdon, Nock, Twigg, Mortimer, Joseph Manton, John Manton, Purdey (*7, 8, 10, 11, 38, 136–8*).

East India Company   Military-pattern firearms are often encountered bearing the lion crest or bale mark of the company, and a date.

Egg   The Egg family were renowned English makers of fine firearms from the middle of the eighteenth century to the mid-nineteenth century. Durs Egg was the most famous and he made the Ferguson rifle and other military firearms, in addition to a series of high-quality double-barrelled and other pistols (*36*).

Ejector   A mechanism on a gun or pistol which ejects the spent cartridge(s), usually when the action is opened.

Enfield   Enfield Lock, Middlesex, was the site of the Royal Small Arms Manufactory. For fifty years the weapons produced were mostly assembled from parts supplied by contractors. Then, during the 1850s machinery was installed and the factory produced the well-known Enfield percussion rifle and subsequently other models.

Eprouvette   An instrument for testing gunpowder. Various types are found, the most common being of pistol form with a scaled wheel which indicates the power of the powder (*148, 149*).

Escutcheon   A small plate inlet on a firearm stock, usually silver and often ornamental, upon which the owner's crest or initials were engraved.

Etching   A form of decoration on a weapon, obtained by the use of acid.

False Breech   Also known as Hook Breech. A feature on later flintlock, and percussion, firearms whereby the barrel was easily detachable for cleaning. The barrel was secured to the stock by cross bolts passing through loops on its underside, and a hook on the breech plug fitted into a slot in the false breech, which was attached to the stock.

Feather Spring   See *Frizzen Spring*.

Ferguson Rifle   A breech-loading military flintlock rifle having a quick-threaded plug entering the breech vertically. This was attached to the front of the trigger-guard, which acted as a lever, one turn of which lowered the plug to enable the charge to be inserted in the resulting aperture in the top of the barrel. The Ferguson rifle dates from the last quarter of the eighteenth century and examples are found made by Durs Egg.

Firelock   An old term which refers to various types of firearm mechanism.

Fishtail Butt   A self-explanatory term, being a pistol with a butt of fishtail form. Some Irish pistols by Rigby, and other makers, had this shape of butt.

Flash Pan   The concave pan beside the touch-hole of a flintlock or matchlock firearm in which the flash powder is ignited in order to fire the charge. See also *Rainproof Pan*.

Flint   The flint held between the jaws of a pistol or gun cock makes a spark as it strikes against the frizzen (or steel), and this ignites the touch powder.   Gun flints are still knapped at Brandon in Suffolk.

Lock Plate   *Feather or Frizzen Spring*

Jaw Screw
Top Jaw
Steel or Frizzen   *Pan*   *Cock Bridle*
Pan Cover
Main Spring   *Bent   Sear*
Tumbler

Flintlock   A type of firearm mechanism in which a piece of flint, held in the jaws of the cock, is struck against a steel, or frizzen, producing sparks which ignite the flash powder in the pan, which in turn fires the charge (*27–32, 144*).

Fore-end   The front portion of the stock of a firearm, i.e. the part in front of the lock. It often has a tip, or end cap, of horn, brass or silver.

Forsyth   Alexander John Forsyth was the inventor of the percussion system for igniting firearms. He was born in 1768, son of a minister, whose calling he followed. His hobbies were shooting, chemistry and mechanical engineering, and he experimented to try and produce a better and alternative system to the flintlock. By 1807 he had invented the 'scent-bottle' primer lock, so called because the magazine containing the fulminate priming powder was shaped like a scent bottle. This magazine allowed a small amount of fulminate to be released at a time and this was detonated by a flat-nosed hammer. A later variety had a sliding magazine fitted to the lock.

Fountain-pen Pistol   A single-shot pistol disguised as a fountain pen or pencil. They are often considered to be assassin's weapons.

Fowling Piece   A muzzle-loading gun intended for shooting wildfowl. Many fine examples were made by famous English gunmakers. They were usually fullstocked and had high-quality silver or brass mounts. The stocks were sometimes finely inlaid with silver-wire scrollwork.

Frizzen   The steel plate on a flintlock mechanism (*q.v.*) against which the flint strikes, to produce sparks to ignite the charge. It usually also serves as a cover to the flash pan and is sometimes referred to as the 'steel'.

Frizzen Spring   The small V-shaped spring on the outside of a flintlock mechanism (*q.v.*) upon which the frizzen (*q.v.*) bears. Also known as the 'Feather Spring'.

Full-stock   A type of pistol or gun stock which extends right to the muzzle of the weapon.

Furniture   The mounts of a pistol or gun, i.e. trigger guard, butt cap or plate, sideplate and escutcheon. Generally of steel, brass or silver and frequently engraved or chiselled. On English late seventeenth- and early eighteenth-century examples the motif was often of strawberry leaves, monster's heads, etc. In the mid-eighteenth century the designs were of acanthus and trophies of arms. The butt caps of pistols were frequently in the form of grotesque masks. Trigger-guard finials were designed as acorns, and later as pineapples or urns.

Fuse Pistol A pistol made to ignite the fuse used by Army sappers to explode land mines, for blasting, etc. Percussion and centre-fire models were made, the former of brass construction dating from about 1880.

Fusil A light form of flintlock musket carried by sergeants and officers.

Game Counter A pocket indicator for keeping a record of the total game bagged during a shoot. They are often of brass or German silver and have ratchet indicators on numbered dials for pheasants, partridges, hares and rabbits.

Gang Mould A bullet mould (*q.v.*) made to cast a quantity of bullets at the same time.

Garniture A matching set of weapons, i.e. a pair of pistols, gun and powder flask all with decoration *en suite*.

Gravity Feed An early form of repeating cartridge firearm in which the cartridges were contained in an open-sided magazine on the top of the barrel. A rising breech block was attached to the hammer and as this was raised the weapon was pointed upward to permit a cartridge to fall down into the breech (*115*).

Grenade Thrower A gun fitted with a cup at the muzzle, or on the butt, made to fire grenades.

Gun A longarm having a smooth-bore barrel from which shot is fired (*191, 193, 197, 200*).

Gunpowder A mixture of potassium nitrate (saltpetre, or nitre), sulphur and charcoal, used for the explosive charge in firearms from the earliest times.

Hair Trigger or **Set Trigger** A device which enables the firearm to be fired by only a light trigger pull in order to save deflecting the aim.

Half-cock The safety position in a firearm mechanism, between the fired and full-cock positions, when the hammer or cock cannot be released by pulling the trigger.

Half-stock The stock of a firearm which terminates about half-way between the lock and the muzzle.

Hammerless A type of lock action where the striking mechanism is concealed within the frame of the firearm.

Hand Cannon The earliest type of gun having a barrel tube with a touch hole and a straight handle. It was hand ignited with a burning match.

Hand Mortar A short gun with large-bore mortar barrel and conventional gun butt.

Hand-rotated A revolving firearm on which the cylinder or barrels are rotated manually (*85*).

Harmonica Pistol A multi-shot weapon with a number of barrels, in line, in a moving block which resembles a harmonica (*156*).

Harpoon Gun A heavy-barrelled gun of large bore used in whaling to fire a harpoon (*186, 187*).

Heart Butt A double-lobed form of butt found on Scottish Lowland pistols of the seventeenth and eighteenth centuries (*147*).

Hidden Trigger See *Concealed Trigger*.

Highland Pistol A Scottish all-metal pistol with distinctive ramshorn scrolled butt. A pricker with ball terminal was usually fitted between the scrolls. The stock was generally of steel, frequently inlaid with silver scrollwork, and engraved. It had a ball trigger and was fitted with a belt hook (*15*). Later 'dress' pistols with flintlock or percussion locks were also made with ramshorn butts (*17, 18*).

Holster A container, usually of leather, for the pistol or revolver. It can be worn on the belt or carried on horseback.

Holster Pistol   A pistol about 15 to 20 inches in length which was intended to be carried in a holster (*19–23, 27, 151–4*).

Horse Pistol   See *Holster Pistol.*

Howdah Pistol   A heavy holster pistol of the type carried by the hunter on a howdah, for close-range use against wild animals attacking the elephant. Percussion types were usually single-barrelled. The later cartridge weapons were double-barrelled side-by-side.

Jacob   General John Jacob invented a form of rifling with four deep grooves. The Jacob's rifle had double barrels 24 inches long and was fitted with a sword bayonet with pierced design to the knuckle guard. It was not adopted by the Government, but in 1858 two infantry regiments, formed by the inventor, were issued with it.

Jaw Screw   The screw which tightens the jaws of a flintlock (*q.v.*) or wheel-lock cock in order to hold the flint or pyrites secure.

Jezail   An Afghan matchlock or flintlock gun with slender curved butt. Sometimes a forked rest is hinged to the forestock.

Kentucky (Pennsylvania) Rifle   A distinctive type of American rifle developed about 1725. It had a stock of curly maple with pronounced downward-sloping butt. The mounts were usually of brass with an elaborate patch box, and sometimes silver plaques were inlaid in the butt (*201, 202*).

Kerr   The Kerr's patent percussion revolver was of a distinctive design, having a sidehammer mechanism of the back-action type, designed to be easy to service. The revolver was produced by the London Armoury Co., in 54-bore and 80-bore sizes, both in double action and single action. The patent dates of this weapon were 17 December 1858 and 26 January 1859 (*78*).

Ketland, William   A famous Birmingham gunmaker of the second half of the eighteenth century. He produced many fine guns, and manufactured parts for other gunsmiths.

Key Pistol   A form of hand-ignited or matchlock pistol combined with a key, the barrel being the hollow stem of the key. They were thought to have been used by gaolers, but most specimens seen are modern conversions to old keys (*116*).

Knife-pistol   A combined pistol and clasp knife used by gold prospectors and others. A well-known firm of makers was Unwin & Rodgers of Sheffield and their product was named the *Self Protector.* Both percussion and rimfire specimens were produced (*158*). Some European double-barrelled percussion knife-pistols were made, with a barrel down each side of the blade, the split cross-guard acting as the hammers. Pinfire revolvers with a blade beneath the barrel are sometimes found.

Lancaster   Charles Lancaster was a mid-nineteenth-century London gunsmith famous for his patent oval smooth-bore rifling (i.e. the bore was of oval section with a twist, but had no distinct lands or grooves). He also made a series of two- and four-barrelled 'hammerless' pistols with an internal revolving striker.

Lands   The raised sections between the rifling of a firearm barrel.

Lanyard   A cord attached to a firearm at one end, and to the person or saddle at the other end, to prevent its being dropped and lost, particularly when mounted. On revolvers and pistols the lanyard is usually attached to a ring, or swivel, on the butt. On carbines it is affixed to the 'saddle bar' opposite the lock. The term lanyard is also given to the cord which is pulled to fire a cannon lock.

Lanyard Ring   A ring, or swivel mount, on the butt of a pistol or revolver, to which the lanyard (*q.v.*) is attached.

Lefaucheux   A maker of pinfire (*q.v.*) pistols, revolvers and guns, who is sometimes given the credit of having invented this system of ignition.

Le Mat   Colonel Le Mat was the mid-nineteenth-century inventor of the patent revolver which had an extra shot barrel set in the centre of the cylinder. It was made on both the percussion and breech-loading systems (*99, 100*).

Lemon Butt   A form of butt found on some wheel-lock pistols, also on Scottish seventeenth-century snaphaunce pistols.

Loading Mallet   A mallet, often seen in cased sets of muzzle-loading pistols or rifles, and used to help load the bullet into the bore.

Lock   The mechanism by which a firearm is fired. (See *Matchlock, Wheel-lock, Flintlock* and *Percussion*.)

Lock Plate   The metal plate upon which the working parts of the lock mechanism are mounted. It usually bears the maker's name (see *Flintlock*).

Lowland Pistol   A form of Scottish all-metal pistol with a lobe or heart-shaped butt (*16, 147*).

Magazine Gun   A gun fitted with a magazine or magazines to contain a number of charges, primers and bullets, in order to fire repeated charges. Early examples were by Kalthoff, Lorenzoni, Cookson (*q.v.*), etc. Later types were the Volcanic, Henry, Winchester, etc.

Main Spring   The spring, usually of long V shape, which operates the cock or hammer of a firearm.

Manhattan   The Manhattan Firearms Co. of New York and Newark, New Jersey, produced percussion pepperboxes and single-action percussion revolvers. The patent dates of the latter were 27 December 1859 and 8 March 1864, and they resembled the Colt Navy model 1851.

Manton   Joseph Manton (1760–1835) was one of the most famous gunsmiths of the late eighteenth and early nineteenth centuries. He produced high-quality duelling pistols and other firearms, and patented several improvements to firearms design. John Manton, the elder brother of Joseph, also made many fine firearms (*136*).

Mask Butt   A form of butt cap on eighteenth-century pistols designed as a grotesque human face.

Matchlock   The earliest type of mechanism used on firearms. It had a pivoted serpentine holder in which a slow-burning match was secured. The holder hinged down to ignite the flash powder in the pan (*108, 141, 174, 177, 196*).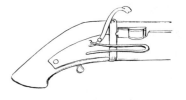

Maynard Tape Primer   A system of percussion ignition patented in 1845 in which a roll of caps (similar to those used on a present-day toy pistol) was used. The roll was fitted in a magazine and was rotated as the weapon was cocked.

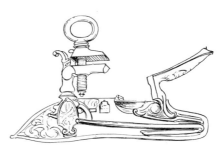

Miquelet Lock   A type of firearms lock, generally Spanish in origin, having an external main-spring and cock, and a horizontal sear which emerges through the lock plate to act on the base of the cock. Both flintlock and percussion actions are found, the former usually with a ring on the top of the jaw screw (*19, 97, 142, 180, 191–3*).

Monkey-tail   The name given to the hinge-up breech block of the Westley Richards patent breech-loading rifle, by reason of its shape. Both percussion and centre-fire models were made.

Muff Pistol   The term often used to describe a small flintlock or percussion boxlock pocket pistol of less than 5 inches in length (*33, 35*).

Multi-barrelled   A firearm with three or more barrels. Various groupings are seen and the following items fall within the term: pepperbox, volley gun, mob pistol and tap-action pistols.

Musket   A military shoulder arm with smooth-bore barrel of large calibre (ten bore on most British weapons) (*194, 195*).

Musket Rest   A forked rest used with early muskets by virtue of their weight. It consisted of a U-shaped metal mount on a pole, supporting the weapon at shoulder level.

Musketoon   A short form of musket having a smooth-bore barrel of large calibre.

Muzzle   The end of a firearm barrel farthest from the breech and from which the charge emerges.

Muzzle-loader   A firearm which is loaded at the muzzle, or the mouth of the chambers in the case of a revolver.

Navy Colt   The well-known Colt percussion revolver, model 1851. It was a six-shot calibre ·36 weapon, 13 inches in length with a barrel of 7½ inches. The cylinder had an engraved naval engagement scene. It was made in both USA and England (*48, 71*). See *Colt*.

Needle-fire   An early type of cartridge firearm, usually breech-loading, wherein the striker is a needle which hits a primer set within the cartridge. Well-known makers were Dreyse and Needham (*93*).

Nipple   The small vented screw-in plug in the breech of a percussion firearm upon which the fulminate cap is placed and through which the charge is ignited on the fall of the hammer.

Nipple Key   A small spanner used to remove and replace the nipples on percussion firearms (*227*).

Nipple Primer   A device used to clear the vent of a percussion nipple that is clogged with burnt gunpowder. The usual variety is a small brass cylinder having a pricker to clear the vent and then a means of dispensing a new supply of powder to re-prime the weapon.

Nock, Henry   A famous gunmaker of the late eighteenth century, renowned for his seven-barrelled volley guns and patent screwless enclosed lock. He made all types of firearms and many examples survive.

Officer's Pistol   A term given to the service type of flintlock or percussion holster pistol, often of musket bore and of somewhat plain finish (*9, 154*).

Over-and-under   A double-barrelled firearm having the barrels superimposed one over the other, as opposed to side-by-side (*29, 123, 124*).

Palm Pistol   A pistol which can be concealed in the palm of the hand. They are fired by compressing the fist and are sometimes known as 'squeezer' pistols. The Chicago 'Protector' type has a rotary cylinder (*111, 161*).

Pan   See *Flash Pan*.

Pan Cover   A sliding cover on wheel-lock and snaphaunce locks which retained the flash powder in the pan until the weapon was fired. (See also *Frizzen*.)

Parker   William Parker was the founder of a well-known firm of gunmakers in Holborn, London. He made flintlock and percussion pistols for the police. The firm later became Parker, Field & Co., then 'and Sons'. All types of firearms were produced, including some patent transition-type percussion revolvers.

Patchbox   A small compartment in the butt of a rifle in which patches were kept. The patch was a piece of material which was wrapped around the ball in order to hold it firmly in the bore. Patch boxes on English weapons had a hinged metal cover *en suite* with the mounts. Those on Continental firearms usually had sliding wooden covers.

Patch-lock   An early type of percussion firearm in which a paper-covered fulminate cap was placed in the nose of the hammer, and was struck on the nipple as the hammer fell. Patchlock weapons usually had detachable strikers, or hammer noses, and a supply of these was carried in a separate case (*206*).

Paterson Colt   A rare and valuable early model of Colt revolver with folding trigger and no trigger guard (*49*). See *Colt*.

Patron   An early type of cartridge container, in the form of a box with a hinged lid. It had vertical compartments and was worn on the belt. The Patron was often inlaid with staghorn, etc., in similar designs to the gun or pistol.

Pauly　　Jean Samuel Pauly took out a French patent, on 29 September 1812, for a breech-loading gun in which a separate self-contained cartridge was used. The cartridge was reloadable and had centre-fire ignition. This was the first example of a firearm in which the primer and the charge were combined.

Pepperbox　　A multi-barrelled firearm, usually a revolver, each barrel being discharged separately. Some similar weapons with fixed barrels and rotating hammers or strikers are also classed as pepperboxes. The earliest pepperbox firearms date back to the seventeenth century, but these are so rare that they are not likely to be encountered outside museums and large collections.

The first well-known type, rare today, is the seven-shot hand-rotated flintlock, with boxlock action, introduced about 1780. Examples of these are found made by Nock, Twigg and Ketland & Co. (*41*).

An early-model English percussion pepperbox revolver was the single-action, boxlock, hand-rotated weapon with vertical nipples and a disc-shaped flash shield at the rear of the barrels. These sometimes had a long spur on the hammer to facilitate the cocking action (*85*). A development of this type was the self-rotating action in which the cylinder revolved as the hammer was cocked.

The final and most common of the percussion models was the self-cocking 'bar hammer' type, also known as the 'top-snap'. In these the action of pulling the trigger turned the cylinder; and the hammer, in form of a horizontal bar along the top of the frame, was raised and then fell to strike the cap (*45, 73, 87–9*).

Various patent pepperboxes were produced, including the Rigby rotating hammer (*q.v.*) (*74*); the J. R. Cooper's patent ring-trigger with underhammer action (*86, 106*); and the Budding, with brass barrels and internal striking action to the horizontal nipples. The last make is probably the rarest of the English pepperboxes, and somewhat of a mystery surrounds its manufacture.

In America the first type encountered is the Darling; a brass-barrelled and brass-framed weapon with hand-rotated single-action operation (*102*). Various bar-hammer models were produced by Ethan Allen and associated companies, Manhattan F.A. Co. and others (*103*); whilst ring-trigger examples, similar to the English Cooper's patent, were made by Blunt & Syms, Robbins & Lawrence, and others.

Small cartridge-firing pepperboxes were later produced on the pinfire (*112*), rimfire and centre-fire systems; and a series of four-barrelled weapons were made by C. Sharps in America, and Tipping & Lawden in England, the latter on Sharps' patent (*167*). These rimfire pistols had a rotating striker on the hammer nose. Charles Lancaster produced a series of four- and two-barrelled holster pistols about 1880. These had an internal rotating centre-fire striker.

Some longarms were made on the pepperbox systems and these are very rare (*171*).

Percussion　　A system of ignition on a firearm in which a cap or primer is struck by a hammer. The Rev. Alexander Forsyth (*q.v.*) invented the first type of percussion system which used fulminate powder. Other inventions followed, including tube ignition, pill-lock, patch-lock, etc. Finally the percussion cap was invented. This was a copper cup, containing a film of fulminate, which was placed over the nipple (*q.v.*).

Percussion Cap　　A method of igniting a percussion firearm. It is a small copper cup-shaped device containing fulminate of mercury, which is placed on the nipple. When the weapon is fired the hammer strikes the capped nipple and the resultant flash through the vent in the nipple ignites the charge in the barrel.

Petronel　　A short firearm of the sixteenth and seventeenth centuries, used mostly by cavalry. It was either a light form of carbine or a long pistol.

Pill-lock or **Pellet-lock**   An early form of percussion ignition using a fulminate pill or pellet. These were contained in a magazine which allowed one at a time to drop into the concave detonating pan. The magazine could be attached to the weapon or be a separate accessory (*114*).

Pinfire   An early type of cartridge ignition, invented just before 1850, in which the cartridge had a detonating pin emerging at right angles to the base. The weapon had a flat-nosed hammer, which when fired struck the pin. The base of the pin then struck the fulminate cap which was contained within the cartridge. Lefaucheux, a French maker, was noted for his pinfire weapons.

Pistol   A hand firearm. Various types could be carried in the pocket, the belt or a holster.

Pocket Pistol   A small pistol, about 6 inches overall, which could be carried in the pocket (*3–5, 28–31, 33–5*).

Poinçon   A maker's mark impressed on the lock or breech of a firearm, sometimes with a ground of gold or platinum.

Powder Flask   A container for gunpowder carried by the sportsman and soldier. The use of powder flasks commenced about 1500 and continued until the end of the muzzle-loading era.

The earliest flasks were made from hollowed-out horns fitted with a stopper. In the sixteenth to eighteenth centuries many fine flasks were produced, often *en suite* with the decoration on the rifle or gun. Some were combined with a key to span the wheel-lock. Flattened horn flasks were engraved with hunting scenes; others made of sections of stag antler were finely carved. These usually had steel or brass mounts and a long conical charger. Others were of turned wood or ivory, carved or inlaid (*233, 234, 236, 243*). The Italian seventeenth-century flasks were often of steel, half conical in form, with fluted sides (*211*).

In the eighteenth and early nineteenth centuries sailors, soldiers and settlers often made their own cowhorn flasks and engraved them with ships, the Royal arms, regimental names, etc. The American colonial powder horns engraved with maps are very rare and valuable (*242*).

The nineteenth century saw the mass production of copper powder-flasks, many embossed with patterns, huntsmen and dogs, birds, dead game, foliage, shell and bush designs, etc. Both gun and pistol size were made, with various patent chargers, and in assorted shapes (*231, 232*).

Pistol flasks known as 'two-way' or 'three-way' were produced, having built-in compartments to hold spare flints or percussion caps, and balls (*229, 230*).

The well-known English makers of this period were Dixon & Sons, Hawksley, Sykes, Bartram, and Frith. Some copper flasks have been reproduced in recent years, and the old patterns have been used.

In the USA the American Flask and Cap Company made large numbers of copper flasks.

A series of flasks were produced in America and England to be sold in cased outfits together with Colt and other firearms. Some of these were embossed with eagle, crossed pistols or military trophies. A rare type of Colt flask was the multiple-charge cylindrical model used with the Paterson revolvers (*q.v.*) (*47–9, 240*).

Some of the desirable English flask designs are the entwined dolphins, gun-stock shape, and 'three horse heads' (*210, 239*).

Powder flasks from many countries are to be found. The Moorish types are circular or horn-shaped brass, engraved and often silver-overlaid, both varieties with two large suspension rings.

Indian flasks are often of curled trumpet shape, pear or fish shape, etc., sometimes with fine mother-of-pearl inlay (*215, 219, 237*).

Persian examples are often of banana shape in steel, damascened, and with a long cut-off lever extending along the body of the flask (*217*).

Good-quality French flasks of embossed copper are seen, often by Boche of Paris; also some of brass-mounted pear-shaped lanthorn (*235*).

The Japanese flask, *hayago*, was made of lacquered wood, papier-mâché or horn.

Powder Magazine   A receptacle used to store gunpowder. The copper containers are often fitted in a mahogany case.

Powder Measure   An implement scaled to measure a set amount of gunpowder (*208, 209*).

Pricker   A needle-like implement used to clear the fouling from a touch hole or nipple. Scottish pistols have a pricker screwed into the butt.

Primer   The means of igniting the main charge. In flintlock and earlier firearms the primer was the fine gunpowder placed in the flash pan. In the percussion system a fulminate cap, pellet, patch or tube was used. In the later cartridge weapons the primer was a cap affixed in the base of the cartridge.

Proof Mark   A mark made by the Gunmakers' Company, on the barrel of a firearm, to indicate that it had passed a proof test of safety.

The proof charge used was usually twice the normal charge. A charter given to the company made illegal the sale of unproved firearms. The London proof marks are a crowned V (the view mark) and a crowned G P monogram (the proof mark). The Birmingham marks after 1813 were a crown over crossed sceptres, one with the letters BPC between the arms, the other a V. The Liège mark is also illustrated.

Punt Gun   A long gun of large bore used by wildfowlers. It was mounted in a punt for use in the shallows or marshes.

Purse Pistol   A pistol or revolver built into the frame of a purse, and used by ladies as a concealed weapon for self-protection. The term is also used to describe a small tiny-calibre pistol carried in the purse.

Queen Anne Pistol   A term given to the distinctive type of flint-lock pistol introduced about the time of Queen Anne in the early eighteenth century. It was an 'overcoat' pocket weapon and had a cannon barrel which could be unscrewed for loading. The frizzen spring was fitted in front of the pan (see *Feather Spring*). Queen Anne pistols were nearly always silver-mounted. The type continued to be made into the third quarter of the eighteenth century (*95, 134*).

Rainproof Pan   A patent flash pan on later flintlocks designed to prevent the rain or damp affecting the priming powder. The pan was V-shaped and the pan cover designed to fit more snugly. Some rainproof pans had a raised rim.

Ramrod   The rod usually fitted beneath the barrel of a firearm used to ram the charge firmly down the bore. It has a flared-out tip for ramming purposes, and the other end is frequently fitted with a 'worm' for removing a misfired charge.

Ramrod Pipes   The small tubular pipes fitted beneath the barrel or stock to hold the ramrod in place, when not in use. The pipe where the ramrod enters the stock is known as the 'throat-pipe'.

Ramshorn Butt   A double-scrolled butt found on Scottish Highland pistols (*15, 17, 18*).

Rat-tail Butt   A slender pointed butt-form found on Albanian metal-stocked Miquelet pistols.

Reloading Tools   Special tools made for reloading cartridges. They were used for capping and decapping; crimping; turning over, etc.

Remington   The Remington Company produced single-action percussion revolvers in ·36 and ·44 calibre, patent dates 14 September 1858 and 17 December 1861. Cartridge pistols, revolvers, derringers, four-shot pistols and longarms were also made (*57, 159*).

Revolver   A multi-shot firearm with a revolving cylinder or barrels. The term generally refers to a pistol with rotating chambers.

Revolving Longarms   Rifles and guns with revolving chambers were made from the earliest times, but wheel-lock and flintlock examples are very rare. Collier made them with flintlock and percussion mechanisms. Colt made percussion specimens at Paterson and Hartford. Various other American and English makers produced percussion revolving longarms. Some cartridge models are also found (*171, 174, 184, 189, 204*).

Rifle   A longarm with a rifled barrel.

Rifling   The spiral grooves cut in the barrel of a firearm in order to make the ball rotate and obtain greater accuracy.

Rigby Rotating Striker   A patent multi-shot percussion pistol or gun with a hand-rotated revolving striker on the nose of the hammer. A separate nipple is provided for each barrel and these are struck in turn. Most specimens known were made by Rigby (*74*).

Rimfire   An early type of metallic cartridge with the detonating charge contained in the rim of the case. The hammer had a flat rectangular striker and the rear of the chamber acted as the anvil (*44*).

Ring-trigger   A trigger in the form of a ring, found on Cooper and Mariette pepperboxes, and some other firearms (*105, 106*).

Saddle Bar   A steel bar, often with a sliding ring, which is fixed to the stock of a carbine at the opposite side to the lock; and to which a lanyard is affixed, to prevent the weapon being lost, if dropped.

Safety Catch   A device engaging the mechanism of a firearm to ensure against accidental discharge. Various forms are found, mostly bolting the cock or hammer.

Saloon Pistol   A single-barrelled pistol of small bore designed for indoor target practice.

Saw-handle Butt   A style of butt found on some late flintlock duelling pistols and percussion pistols, including the bootleg type. The top of the butt had an extension, similar to that on a saw handle, and enabled a firmer grip to be taken.

Schuetzen   A distinctive type of Austrian rifle with a heavy 'crook' butt. It had a large scrolled trigger guard and double set-trigger action.

Scottish Pistol   An all-metal belt pistol of distinctive type. See *Highland Pistol* and *Lowland Pistol* (*15, 18, 147*).

Screw Barrel   Correctly this means a rifled barrel. The term is, however, often used to define a turn-off barrel (*q.v.*) (*32*).

Sear or **Scear**   The small pivot in a lock mechanism acting between the trigger and the tumbler. The wedge-shaped end engages in the bents (*q.v.*), or notches, in the tumbler and the angled end is operated by the trigger. See *Flintlock*.

Sea Service Pistol   A brass-mounted military-pattern flintlock or percussion pistol, usually fitted with a belt hook, for use on board ship, or by coastguards. Two British flintlock models were made, the long pattern 18 inches overall, barrel 12 inches, and the short pattern 15 inches, barrel 9 inches; both of ·56 calibre. The percussion model was 11½ inches overall, with a 6-inch barrel of ·567 calibre. The latter had a swivel ramrod and lanyard ring on the butt.

Segallas   A type name given to a series of eighteenth-century all-steel cannon-barrelled flintlock boxlock pocket pistols. They were about 5 inches in length, and two- and four-barrelled specimens are found in addition to the single-barrel variety. These pistols were probably made in Belgium, but many were signed 'Segallas, London', hence the type name (*130*).

Self-cocking   A revolver action in which the hammer was raised and the cylinder rotated by the act of pulling the trigger. When the hammer reached a certain point it then fell to strike the nipple. This mechanism is found on the 'bar' hammer pepperboxes and the Adams model 1851 revolver, in addition to a series of Birmingham-made percussion revolvers.

Serpentine   The moving arm on the lock of a matchlock firearm which held the slow-burning match. When the trigger was pulled the serpentine pivoted down to the flash pan to ignite the touch powder (*177*).

Set Trigger   See *Hair Trigger*.

Shot Charger   A metal container, often double-ended, in which a set charge of shot was contained for quick and accurate reloading in the field.

Shot Flask   A container for lead shot, generally of leather, bag-shaped and with a cut-off charger to measure a set amount of shot. Sometimes the shot flask is in the form of a shoulder belt and occasionally a double-charger variety is found.

Side-by-side   A firearm with two barrels side-by-side. It usually had two locks, also side-by-side, sometimes with a single trigger operating first one lock and then the other (*6, 145*).

Sidelock   A lock mechanism fitted at the side of the firearm, which can be removed complete.

Sideplate   A metal plate, frequently ornamental, fitted on the opposite side of the stock to the lock, and serving as a guide plate and washer for the lock-retaining bolts, or side-nails.

Signal Pistol   A pistol of large bore designed to fire a signal flare.

Sind Butt   See *Afghan Butt*

Single-action   A revolver action in which the hammer is cocked by the thumb spur. On all except the earliest pepperboxes, the cylinder rotates at the same time. The trigger is then pulled to fire the weapon (*76, 78, 85*).

Skeleton Butt   A type of butt fitted to a firearm in order to re-duce the weight. It could be a conventional wooden stock with the centre cut out, or a thin metal framework. Detachable skeleton butts were made to fit pistols and walking-stick guns, to convert them to shoulder weapons (*55, 198*).

Sling   A leather or webbing strap attached to the butt and fore-end of a longarm, and by means of which it was carried slung over the shoulder.

Sling Swivels   Steel loops on the butt and fore-end of a rifle or gun to which the sling (*q.v.*) is attached.

Smith & Wesson   This famous company started with the manu-facture of Volcanic repeating pistols (*q.v.*); but the first revolvers made were a series of single-action rimfire weapons. Many different models of cartridge handguns followed, and the company is still producing quality firearms.

Snaphaunce   An early form of lock in which a cock holding a piece of flint or pyrites strikes a steel which hinges verti-cally over the pan. The steel is not com-bined with the pan cover as in the later flintlock (*129*).

Spanner   The tool for 'spanning' or winding the wheel of the wheel-lock mechanism. It is often combined with a screwdriver or powder measure, or may be fitted to a powder flask.

Spring Bayonet   A hinged bayonet fitted to the barrel of some blunderbusses, pistols, carbines, etc., which was spring-loaded to fly forward and lock into the 'ready' position when required (*30, 170*). It was patented by Waters & Co. of Birmingham in 1776.

Spring Vice   A clamp for compressing the springs of a firearm. It is often found as an accessory in good-quality cased outfits.

Spur-trigger   A form of trigger set in an extension of the frame, and not having a guard. It is found on some early cartridge revolvers and derringer pistols.

Starr Percussion Revolvers   The Starr Arms Co., New York, produced ·36 and ·44 percussion revolvers, the first in double action, the latter both single and double action. They had a hinged loading lever beneath the barrel. The patent date was 15 January 1856.

Steel   See *Frizzen.*

Stock   The main body of the firearm on which the barrel, lock and mounts are fitted. The stock is usually of wood, but sometimes metal is used.

Suma   The Turkish pistol ramrod. It was suspended from the belt by a swivel loop and often contained tweezers or a dagger. The suma was frequently ornamental and made to match the pistol.

Sundial Gun   See *Alarm Gun.*

Superimposed Load   A firearm in which two or more charges are set one behind the other in a single barrel. The charges are fired one at a time by means of a series of locks and touch holes (or nipples) or a sliding lock (*56*).

Swivel Ramrod   A ramrod attached to the muzzle of a firearm by means of a swivel link, the purpose being to prevent loss of the ramrod, particularly when on horseback. It is also known as a stirrup ramrod (*152, 154*).

Sword-pistol   A combination weapon in which a pistol action is mounted in the hilt of a sword. The barrel lies alongside the blade at the forte, and the grip of the hilt serves as the butt of the pistol. Examples are found with various types of ignition and some were in the form of a revolver (*26*).

Tap Action   A device fitted to a multi-barrelled pistol which enables one selected barrel to be discharged at a time. The 'tap' is set in the base of the flash pan and is rotated into set positions which link a series of touch holes to the respective barrels (*29, 94*).

Tape Primer   A form of percussion ignition in which a roll of paper caps, similar to the present-day toy-pistol caps, is contained in a magazine on the lock. As the hammer is cocked the roll of caps moves and a new cap emerges above the nipple. The Maynard tape primer was fitted to various American firearms following its invention in 1845.

Toby Pistol   A term sometimes given to the chubby late seventeenth-century pocket pistols with bulbous butts.

Top-hat Cap   A form of percussion cap shaped like a top hat. It was used on a special type of pistol having a hinged ring cover over the nipple, which served to retain the cap.

Toradar   An Indian matchlock gun. It has a fullstock and slender, straight, flat-sided butt. The barrel is held to the stock by a number of bands, usually metal and frequently ornamental (*177*).

Touch Hole   The small hole through the breech linking the flash pan with the charge in the chamber, and through which the charge is ignited.

Tower   The marking TOWER (i.e. Tower of London) together with the monarch's crowned cypher GR, VR, etc., is found on many British service weapons of the flintlock and percussion periods (*122, 152, 194, 195*).

Trade Gun   A cheap form of musket or gun, generally with a long 'gas pipe' barrel, fullstock and iron mounts. These were traded with the natives, who often embellished them with brass nails. The locks frequently bear an impressed 'elephant' mark and the word 'Warranted'.

Trade Label   A label often found in the lid of a firearm case. It gives the maker's name and address, sometimes illustrations of his patent, and loading instructions (*53*).

Transition Revolver   A form of percussion revolver having the self-cocking top-snap action of a pepperbox revolver, but with a separate barrel attached to the cylinder pin, and sometimes the lower frame. It was a transitional weapon between the pepperbox and the true revolver (*54, 76*).

Tranter   William Tranter of Birmingham was a prolific maker of percussion revolvers, early cartridge revolvers, and single-shot target pistols. One of his well-known patents, in 1853, was a double-trigger action on the revolvers. The lower trigger cocked the hammer and the upper trigger, within the guard, fired the revolver, or could be used for double action (*55*). The rimfire revolver was patented in 1868 (*44*).

Travelling Pistol   A medium-sized pistol about 9 inches overall. It could have a boxlock action usually with side hammer (or cock), or have a sidelock action and fullstock (*6, 121*).

Trigger   The small lever, usually beneath the lock, which is pulled to activate the mechanism of a firearm. On a few weapons, e.g. certain walking-stick guns, the trigger is a button which is pressed.

Trigger Guard   A looped guard, generally of metal, which protects the trigger and saves accidental discharge.

Tschinke   A Bohemian seventeenth-century light wheel-lock rifle used for bird shooting. The butt-stock has a distinctive curve, and the mainspring and chain are visible below the lock.

Tube-lock   An early percussion lock in which the primer was a thin tube of copper containing fulminate. The tube was either laid on an 'anvil' with one end in the touch hole, or inserted in a special type of nipple with large vent. Joseph Manton of London patented the former system in 1818.

Tumbler   The pivoting member of a lock mechanism to which the cock or hammer is attached externally. Inside the lock the mainspring bears on the tumbler and the sear (*q.v.*) engages in the bents (*q.v.*) which are cut in its base. See *Flintlock*.

Turn-off Barrel   A firearm in which the barrel was unscrewed for loading. See also *Screw Barrel*.

Turn-over   A two- or four-barrelled firearm on which the barrels are hand rotated, or turned over, through 180 degrees to fire the second discharge. A separate pan and frizzen, or nipple, is provided for each barrel (*125, 132*).

Turnpike Gun   A heavy shoulder gun with blunderbuss barrel. Used by toll-gate keepers against highwaymen or other villains.

Twigg, T.   A famous London gunmaker of the second half of the eighteenth century. He made multi-barrelled flintlock pistols of the pepperbox and tap-action types, fine cased duelling pistols, etc.

US Military Pistols   Known as 'Martial' pistols. Many patterns were made both flintlock and percussion, and later, revolvers. They bore US markings, the date, etc., and often the place of manufacture, e.g. Harpers Ferry and Springfield (*66, 118, 119*).

Volcanic   An early type of magazine repeating pistol, or rifle, which fired a lead projectile with the charge contained in its hollow base. It had a lever-action mechanism. The Volcanic Repeating Arms Company was formed in 1855 and was subsequently taken over by Winchester, the rifles developing into the famous series of Winchester lever-action repeaters (*98, 107*).

Volley Gun   A multi-barrelled gun or rifle made to discharge all barrels simultaneously. The best-known examples are those by Henry Nock, who made both military and private weapons (*172*).

Wad Cutter   A steel punch made to cut the wad or patch used with muzzle-loaders.

Walch Percussion Revolver   The Walch Firearms Co., New York, produced a percussion revolver which fired twelve shots. The cylinder had six chambers in which the loads were superimposed. It had twelve nipples, two hammers and two triggers. The patent date was 8 February 1859. A ten-shot model was also made (*56*).

Wall Piece   A heavy gun or rifle fired from a wall, and usually mounted on a swivel. Also known as rampart gun.

Webley   The Webley family are famous for their firearms. The first type of revolver was on the percussion system with a long spur on the hammer, to cock the single action (*53*). Numerous other models followed, a wide and interesting range of cartridge weapons being produced, both for private and service use.

Wheel-lock   An early type of firearm ignition mechanism. The lock had a spring-loaded wheel, with serrated edge, which projected slightly into the flash  pan. A piece of pyrites was held in the jaws of the cock, in contact with the wheel, and when the mechanism was set off by the trigger, the wheel revolved and produced a spark. The wheel-lock dates back to the early sixteenth century and it was in general use until the mid-seventeenth century. It continued in use in Germany for about another hundred years in rifles for hunting and target use (*140, 192*).

Wogdon Robert Wogdon was a renowned late eighteenth-century maker of duelling pistols, with premises in the Haymarket, London. He was a prolific maker and many cased pairs of his pistols are preserved. They were usually of plain form, fullstocked, with steel mounts. Some high-quality silver-mounted pistols were also made. Just before the end of the century John Barton joined in partnership with Robert Wogdon (*10*).

Worm The screw-threaded attachment fitted to the ramrod and used to withdraw a misfired or unspent charge.

1 A pair of short flintlock holster pistols by Stauden-mayer, London, cased with accessories. 11¾″, barrels 6″. *Circa* 1820.

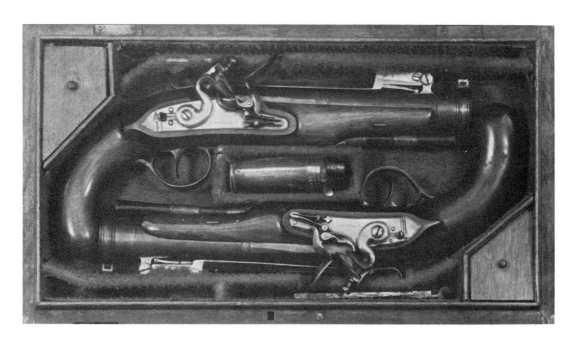

2 A pair of brass-barrelled flintlock blunderbuss pistols by Twigg, London, with top spring-bayonets, cased with accessories. 11½″, barrels 7″. *Circa* 1790.

Cased pairs of English flintlock pistols.

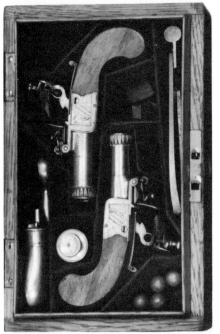

3 A pair of flintlock boxlock pocket pistols by Riviere, London, cased with accessories. $4\frac{1}{2}''$, barrels $1\frac{1}{4}''$. *Circa* 1815.

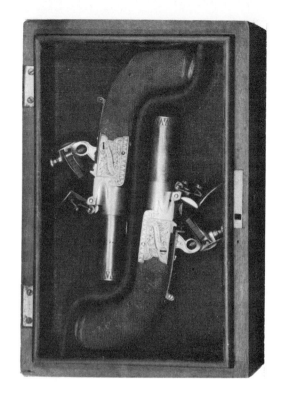

4 A pair of flintlock boxlock pocket pistols by D. Scott, Edinburgh, cased, with accessories in lower tray. $6''$, barrels $1\frac{3}{4}''$. *Circa* 1820.

6 A double-barrelled side-by-side percussion boxlock sidehammer travelling pistol by T. J. Mortimer, London, cased with accessories. $7\frac{1}{2}''$, barrels $3\frac{1}{2}''$. *Circa* 1840.

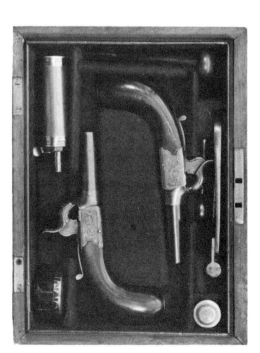

5 A pair of percussion boxlock pocket pistols by Watson, London, cased with accessories. $5\frac{1}{4}''$, barrels $1\frac{1}{2}''$. *Circa* 1840.

Cased sets of flintlock and percussion pistols.

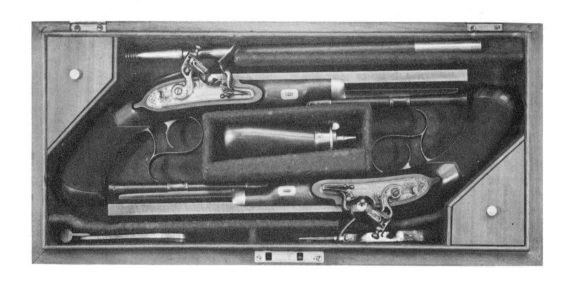

7 A pair of flintlock duelling pistols by James Wilkinson, London, in their case with accessories. 15¼″, barrels 9½″. *Circa* 1815.

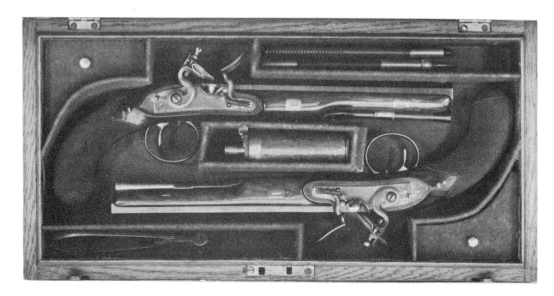

8 A pair of flintlock duelling pistols by Barber & Boaler, Newark, in their case with accessories. 14¾″, barrels 9″. *Circa* 1800.

Cased pairs of English flintlock duelling pistols.

9 A pair of officer's percussion holster pistols by
Gameson, London, cased
with accessories. $15\frac{1}{2}''$,
barrels 10″. *Circa* 1840.

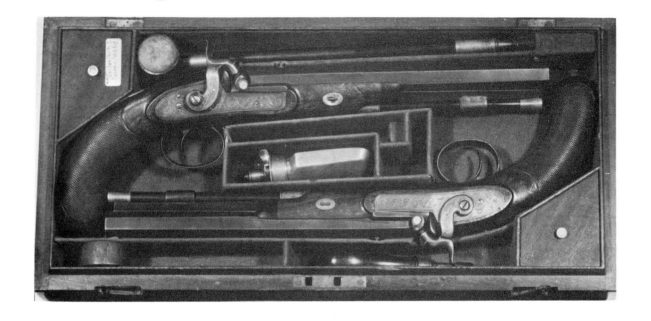

10 A pair of flintlock
duelling pistols by Wogdon,
London, cased with acces-
sories. $14\frac{1}{2}''$, barrels $9\frac{1}{2}''$.
Circa 1790.

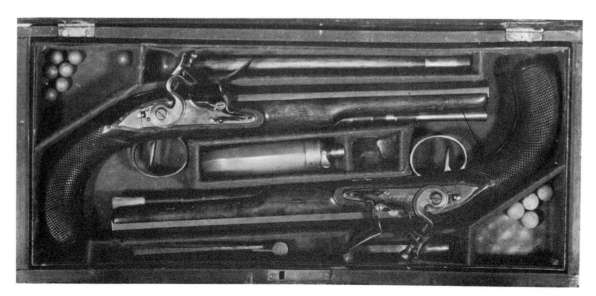

Cased pairs of English pistols.

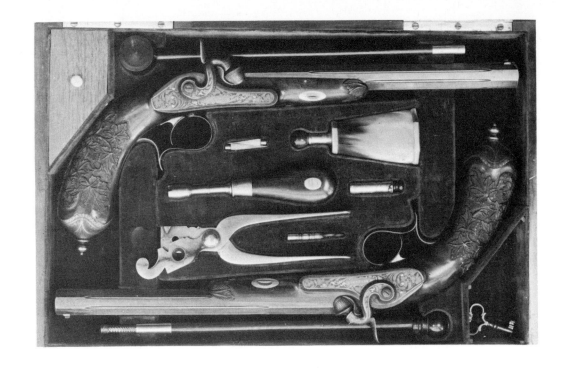

11 A pair of percussion duelling pistols by Peter Schenk of Marienbad, in their fitted case with accessories. 15½", barrels 9½". *Circa* 1840.

12 A cased walking-stick air rifle, complete with pump, bullet mould, keys, etc. 38½" overall, assembled. *Circa* 1850.

13 A ·41 Colt No. 3 Derringer pistol, with ivory grips, in its fitted case. 5", barrel 2½". *Circa* 1880.

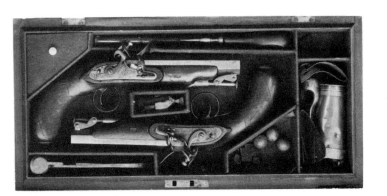

14 A cased pair of flintlock holster pistols by Rigby, Dublin. 10¾", barrels 6". *Circa* 1810.

Cased pistols and air rifle.

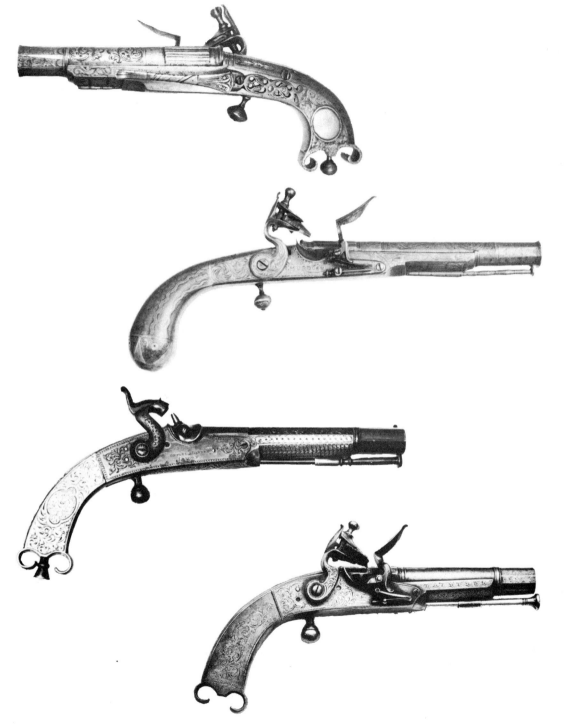

15 Scottish Highland flintlock pistol by Murdoch, with
ramshorn butt. 8″, barrel 5″.
Circa 1770.

16 Scottish Lowland flintlock pistol by Murdoch, with
lobe butt. 14″, barrel 8″.
Circa 1780.

17 Scottish Highland percussion dress pistol by
Tipping & Lawden, London.
11″, barrel 6½″. *Circa* 1850.

18 Scottish Highland flint-
lock dress pistol made in
Birmingham. 10″, barrel 6″.
Early nineteenth century.

Scottish all-metal pistols.

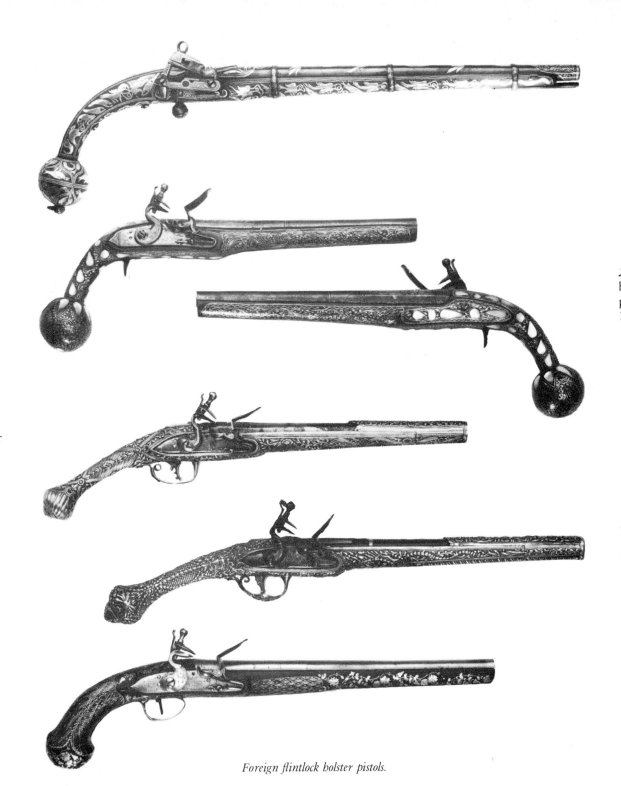

19 A Cossack Miquelet flintlock holster pistol with ball butt. The entire stock of metal overlaid with silver birds and fishes. 17″, barrel 12″. *Circa* 1840.

20 A pair of Balkan ball-butted flintlock holster pistols, with inlaid stocks. 16½″, barrels 11″. *Circa* 1850.

21 A Greek flintlock holster pistol with chased and embossed white-metal stock. 19″, barrel 11″. *Circa* 1840.

22 A Balkan flintlock holster pistol with chased and embossed white-metal stock. 21″, barrel 12½″. *Circa* 1850.

23 A Continental flintlock holster pistol with inlaid stock, made for the Eastern market. 19¾″, barrel 13″. *Circa* 1820.

Foreign flintlock holster pistols.

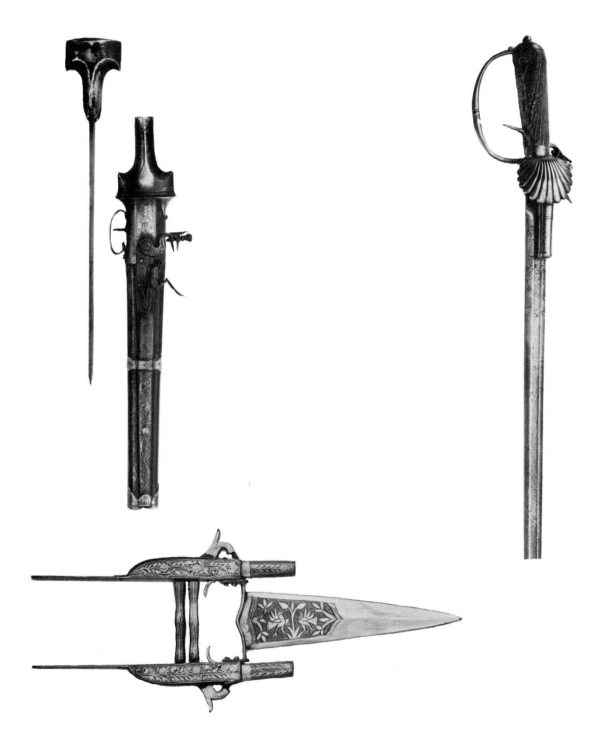

24 An Indian double-barrelled over-and-under flintlock pistol, with dagger in butt. 20″ overall, barrels 10½″, blade 12″. *Circa* 1830.

25 A combined hunting sword and flintlock pistol. Blade 26″. *Circa* 1750.

26 An Indian combined katar and percussion pistol with silver damascened decoration. Blade 10¼″. Mid-nineteenth century.

Combination firearms and edged weapons.

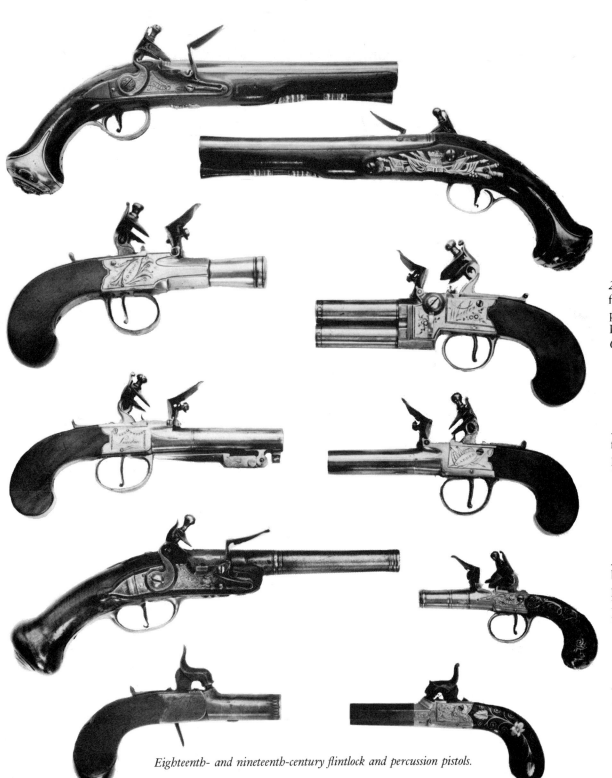

27 A pair of fully silver-mounted flintlock holster pistols by Griffin, London, the mounts with London hallmark for 1756. 13½″ overall, barrels 8″.

28 (left) A brass-barrelled flintlock boxlock blunderbuss pocket pistol by Hill, London. 7″ overall, barrel 3″. *Circa* 1800.

29 (right) A double-barrelled flintlock boxlock tap-action pocket pistol by Wheeler, London. 7½″, barrels 2½″. *Circa* 1790.

30 (left) A flintlock boxlock pocket pistol with spring-bayonet, by Blair, London. 7½″, barrel 3½″. *Circa* 1800.

31 (right) A brass-barrelled flintlock boxlock pocket pistol by Barber, London. 7″, barrel 3″. *Circa* 1800.

32 (left) A French screw-barrelled flintlock sidelock pistol by Turenne. 10″, barrel 6″. Early eighteenth century.

33 (right) A small cannon-barrelled flintlock boxlock pocket pistol by Mortimer, London. The barrel and frame of pale brass, the butt inlaid silver-wire work. 5″, barrel 2″. *Circa* 1770.

34 (left) A percussion box-lock pocket pistol by Wilson, London, with hidden trigger (out). 6″, barrel 2″. *Circa* 1840.

35 (right) A small percussion boxlock pocket pistol by Usherwood, London, with inlaid butt and hidden trigger (in). 5½″, barrel 1¾″. *Circa* 1840.

Eighteenth- and nineteenth-century flintlock and percussion pistols.

36 An English air pistol by Egg, with sphere reservoir. 16″ overall, barrel 10½″. Late eighteenth century.

37 A 4-barrelled flintlock volley pistol by Probin, London. 12″ overall, barrels 4″. *Circa* 1770.

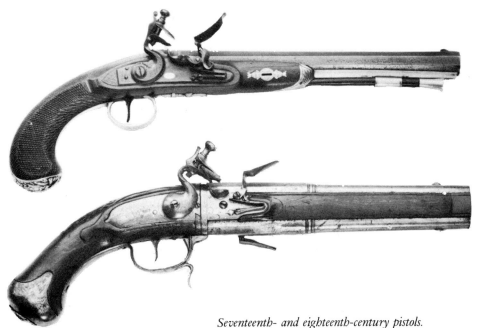

38 A silver-mounted flint-lock duelling pistol by Bate, London, with hallmark for 1783. 15½″ overall, barrel 10″.

39 A Continental double-barrelled turnover flintlock holster pistol of 'Wender' type. 16″ overall, barrels 9″. Late seventeenth century.

Seventeenth- and eighteenth-century pistols.

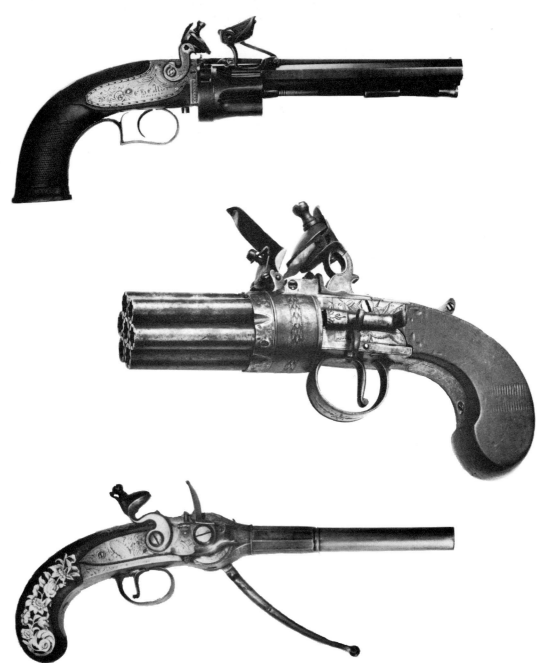

40 A Collier patent flintlock revolver. 14″, barrel 6″. *Circa* 1820.

41 A 7-shot flintlock pepperbox revolver by Nock. 8½″, barrels 2½″. *Circa* 1800.

42 A 'Cookson'-type repeating flintlock pistol by H. W. Mortimer, London. Also known as the Lorenzoni Principle. 15″, barrel 7″. *Circa* 1800.

Multi-shot flintlock pistols.

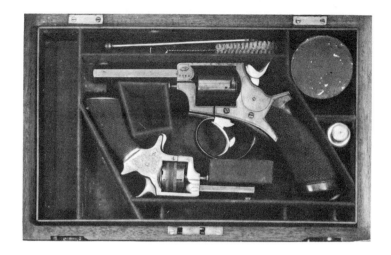

43 A pair of percussion pocket pistols, 5½″, by Westley Richards, London, in unusual upright casing. *Circa* 1840.

44 A ·22 rimfire Tranter single-action revolver, 6¼″, and a ·320 rimfire Tranter double-action revolver, 8½″, cased and retailed by Williams & Powell, Liverpool. *Circa* 1865.

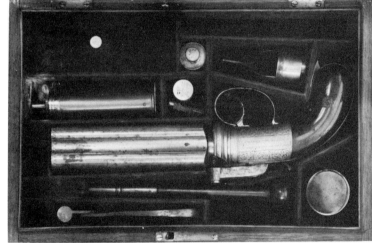

45 A 4-barrelled top-snap percussion pepperbox revolver, 11″, cased with accessories. *Circa* 1850.

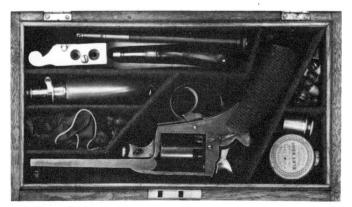

46 A 120-bore Beaumont Adams patent double-action percussion revolver, 9½″, cased with accessories. *Circa* 1860.

Cased percussion and rimfire pistols and revolvers.

47 Cased Colt second model dragoon percussion revolver, with stand-of-flags powder flask, bullet mould, etc. 14″, barrel 7½″. *Circa* 1850.

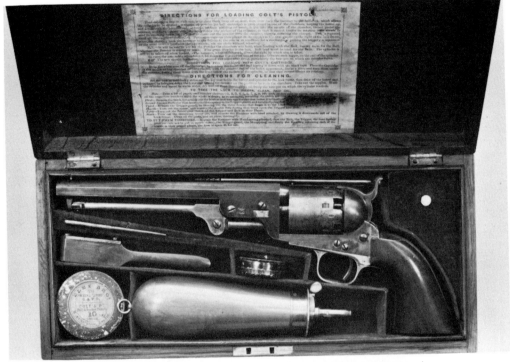

48 A 6-shot ·36 Colt model 1851 Navy percussion revolver, London-made specimen, in English case with accessories. 13″, barrel 7½″.

49 Colt Paterson 5-shot ·31 belt model percussion revolver, No. 615, in its case with spare cylinder, multiple powder flask, bullet mould, cap dispenser and tool. Pistol 9¼″, barrel 5½″. *Circa* 1840.

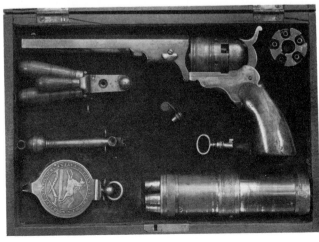

Cased Colt percussion revolvers.

50 Cased Colt model 1860 Army percussion revolver, with detachable shoulder stock, original packets of cartridges, and accessories. Revolver 14″, barrel 8″.

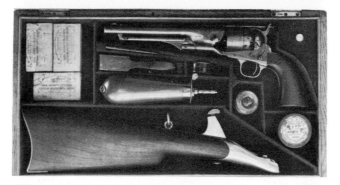

51 A presentation engraved Colt model 1849 pocket percussion revolver, in London case, with accessories. 9″, barrel 4″.

52 A Colt baby dragoon percussion revolver, cased with accessories. 10″, barrel 5″. *Circa* 1848.

Cased Colt percussion revolvers.

53 A Webley patent long-spur hinged wedge-frame single-action percussion revolver, cased with accessories. (Note maker's illustrated trade label.) 13″ overall, barrel 7″. *Circa* 1850.

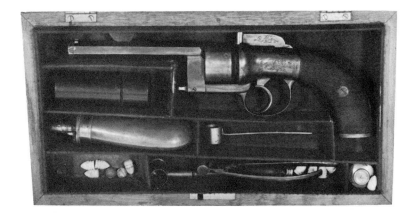

54 A transition percussion revolver by Hollis & Sheath, London, cased with accessories. 11″, barrel 5″. *Circa* 1850.

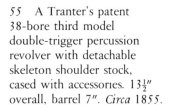

55 A Tranter's patent 38-bore third model double-trigger percussion revolver with detachable skeleton shoulder stock, cased with accessories. 13½″ overall, barrel 7″. *Circa* 1855.

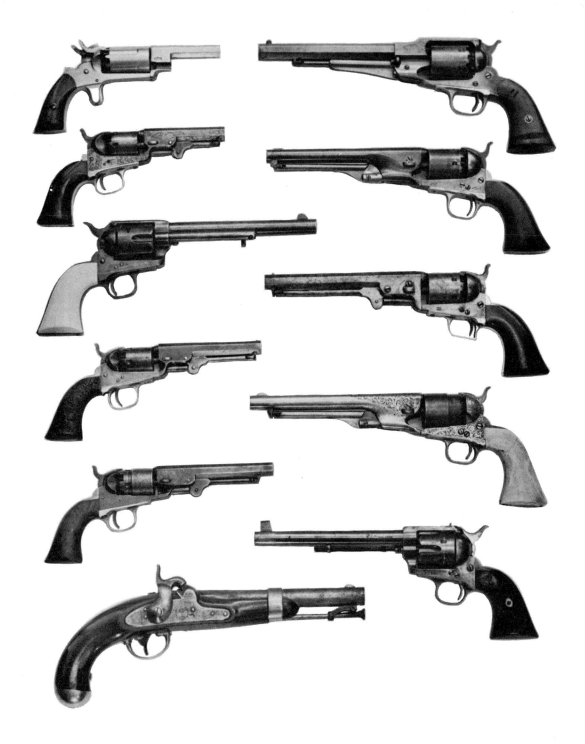

56 A 10-shot Walch Firearms Co. superimposed charge percussion revolver. 8¾", barrel 3¾". *Circa* 1860.

58 A 5-shot ·31 presentation engraved Colt model 1849 pocket percussion revolver. 9", barrel 4".

60 A 6-shot ·45 Colt single-action Army and frontier revolver. 13", barrel 7½". *Circa* 1880.

62 A 5-shot ·31 Colt model 1849 pocket percussion revolver with carved grips. 10", barrel 5".

64 A 5-shot ·36 Colt pocket percussion revolver of Navy calibre. 10½", barrel 5½". *Circa* 1860.

66 A ·54 US model 1842 Palmetto armoury martial percussion pistol. 14¼", barrel 8½".

57 A 6-shot ·44 Remington new model Army percussion revolver. 14", barrel 8". *Circa* 1860.

59 A 6-shot ·36 Colt model 1861 Navy round-barrel percussion revolver. 13" barrel 7½".

61 A 6-shot ·36 Colt model 1851 Navy percussion revolver, early model with square-back trigger guard. 13", barrel 7½".

63 A 6-shot ·44 wolf-engraved Colt model 1860 Army percussion revolver. 13½", barrel 8".

65 A 6-shot ·450 Eley Colt flat-top single-action frontier target revolver. 13", barrel 7½". *Circa* 1890.

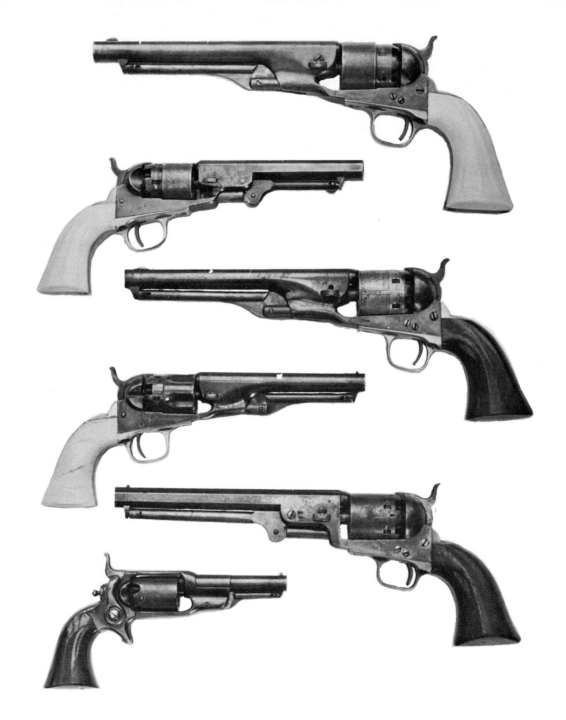

67 Colt model 1860 Army percussion revolver with ivory grips. 14″, barrel 8″.

68 Colt pocket percussion pistol of Navy calibre. 10½″, barrel 5½″. *Circa* 1860.

69 Colt model 1861 Navy percussion revolver, round barrel. 13″, barrel 7½″.

70 Colt model 1862 police percussion revolver with ivory grips. 10½″, barrel 5½″.

71 Colt model 1851 Navy percussion revolver, London made. 13″, barrel 7½″.

72 Colt Root's patent sidehammer model percussion revolver, 1855. 8″, barrel 3½″.

Colt percussion revolvers.

74 A Rigby patent 4-barrelled percussion box-lock pistol with rotating striker. 7″, barrels 2″. *Circa* 1830.

73 A top-snap percussion pepperbox revolver by Horton, Salop. 8″, barrels 3½″. *Circa* 1845.

75 A 5-shot 54-bore Adam's patent 1851 self-cocking percussion revolver with Tranter's patent detachable rammer. 11½″, barrel 6¼″.

76 A 6-shot single-action longspur transition percussion revolver by Witton & Daw, London. 10½″, barrel 4½″. *Circa* 1855.

77 A 5-shot 54-bore Tranter's patent double-action percussion revolver. 12″, barrel 6″. *Circa* 1855.

78 A 5-shot 54-bore Kerr's patent single-action side-hammer percussion revolver. 11″, barrel 5½″. *Circa* 1860.

79 A Colt 6-shot ·31 model 1849 pocket percussion revolver. 11″, barrel 6″.

English and American revolvers.

81 A 54-bore improved model Adam's patent percussion revolver. 11″, barrel 6″. *Circa* 1860.

83 A Belgian copy of a ·44 rimfire Smith & Wesson Russian single-action revolver. 13″, barrel 7¾″. *Circa* 1900.

85 A hand-rotated single-action percussion pepperbox revolver with longspur hammer. 8″, barrel 3½″. *Circa* 1840.

87 A top-snap percussion pepperbox revolver with inlaid butt. 8″, barrels 3″. *Circa* 1845.

89 A top-snap percussion pepperbox revolver with rounded butt. 7½″, barrels 2¾″. *Circa* 1850.

80 A ·44 rimfire Colt single-action Army and frontier revolver. 13″, barrel 7½″. *Circa* 1880.

82 A ·455 British Enfield double-action service revolver, dated 1882. 11½″, barrel 6″.

84 A ·44 Colt third model Hartford English dragoon percussion revolver. 14″, barrel 7½″. *Circa* 1850.

86 A Cooper's patent ring-trigger underhammer percussion pepperbox revolver. 7″, barrel 3″. *Circa* 1840.

88 A good-quality top-snap percussion pepperbox revolver by Braithwaite, Leeds, with top safety and butt trap. 9″, barrels 3¾″. *Circa* 1850.

90 A Belgian 4-barrelled Mariette ring-trigger underhammer percussion pepperbox revolver. 7½″, barrels 2¾″. *Circa* 1850.

Pepperbox and other revolvers.

91 A Colt ·44 Richards conversion on model 1860 Army revolver. 14″, barrel 8″.

92 A US Confederate percussion revolver of Dance Brothers type. 10″, barrel 5″. *Circa* 1864.

93 A 6-shot ·40 Dreyse needle-fire revolver. 12″, barrel 5″. *Circa* 1855.

94 A 3-barrelled flintlock boxlock tap-action pocket pistol. 8″, barrels 3″. *Circa* 1800.

95 A pair of Queen Anne-type silver-mounted flintlock pocket pistols by How, London. 9″, barrels 4½″. *Circa* 1750.

96 An English hand-rotated single-action percussion pepperbox revolver. 8″, barrels 3″. *Circa* 1840.

97 A pair of Spanish Miquelet percussion double-barrelled holster pistols, dated 1849. 12″, barrels 6″.

98 A ·31 volcanic repeating pistol. 9″, barrel 3″. *Circa* 1855.

Miscellaneous pistols and revolvers.

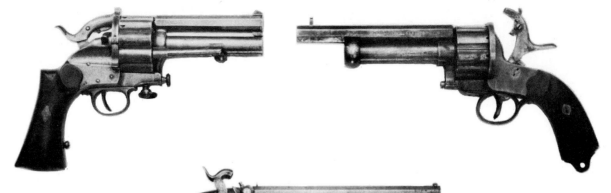

99 A 9-shot 12-mm. centre-fire Le Mat patent single-action revolver. (Note extra-shot barrel below conventional barrel.) 10½", barrels 4½". *Circa* 1870.

100 A Le Mat pinfire revolver. 12½", barrel 6½". *Circa* 1865.

101 A percussion capping breech-loading holster pistol by Lepage, Paris. 14", barrel 8". *Circa* 1850.

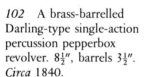

102 A brass-barrelled Darling-type single-action percussion pepperbox revolver. 8½", barrels 3½". *Circa* 1840.

103 A US Allen's patent top-snap self-cocking percussion pepperbox revolver, with ivory grips. 6½", barrels 2¾". *Circa* 1840.

104 An English 4-barrelled hand-rotated single-action percussion pepperbox revolver. 7¾", barrels 2¾". *Circa* 1840.

105 A Belgian 5-barrelled Mariette ring-trigger percussion pepperbox revolver. 7½", barrels 3". *Circa* 1840.

106 A Cooper's patent ring-trigger underhammer percussion pepperbox revolver. 8", barrels 3". *Circa* 1840.

107 A ·30 volcanic repeating pistol. 9", barrel 3½". *Circa* 1855.

Pepperbox revolvers and interesting pistols.

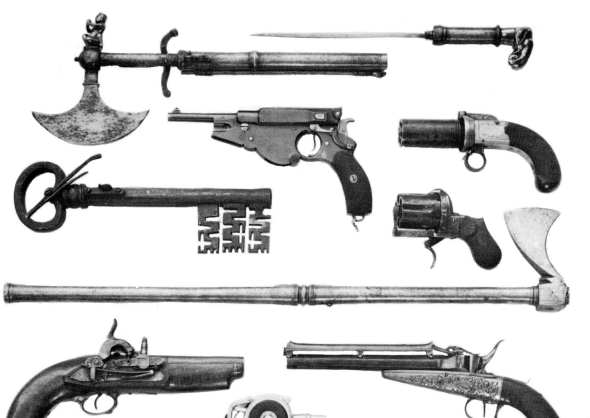

108 An Indian combined axe and matchlock pistol, with screw-in dagger. 22″, barrel 9½″.

110 A top-snap percussion pepperbox revolver with ring-trigger. 8″, barrels 3″. *Circa* 1850.

112 A pinfire pepperbox revolver. 5½″, barrels 2″. *Circa* 1860.

109 (centre) A 6·5-mm. Bergmann 1894 model automatic pistol. 10″, barrel 4½″.

111 A matchlock key pistol. 12½″.

113 An Indian hand-ignited axe-pistol. 28″.

114 A Spanish pill-lock pistol with sliding magazine primer. 12″, barrel 6½″. *Circa* 1830.

116 A protector palm pistol. 5″, barrel 1¾″. *Circa* 1885.

115 A Belgian gravity-feed pistol. 14½″, barrel 9″. *Circa* 1870.

117 A flintlock cannon igniter. 22″. *Circa* 1800.

Firearms curiosa.

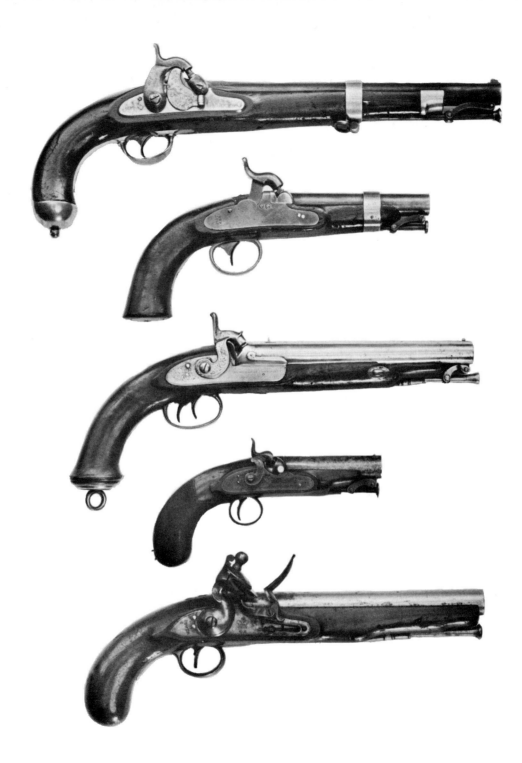

118 A US Springfield model 1855 percussion pistol carbine (without shoulder stock). 18″, barrel 12″.

119 A US contract model 1843 Naval percussion pistol. 12″, barrel 6″.

120 A double-barrelled military percussion holster pistol inscribed, 'Hyderabad Contingent 4th Regt. Cavalry'. 15½″, barrels 9″. *Circa* 1850.

121 An Irish percussion travelling pistol by W. & J. Rigby, Dublin. 9″, barrel 4″. *Circa* 1840.

122 A British 1796 pattern heavy dragoon flintlock holster pistol, the lock marked TOWER and crown over G.R. 15½″, barrel 9″.

Military pistols.

123 A double-barrelled over-and-under flintlock holster pistol by Hewson, London, with swivel ramrod. 11½″, barrels 6″. *Circa* 1810.

124 A double-barrelled over-and-under percussion pistol by H. W. Mortimer, London, with boxlock side-hammer actions. 10½″, barrels 5½″. *Circa* 1830.

125 A 4-barrelled turnover percussion boxlock side-hammer pistol by Manton & Co., Calcutta. 10½″, barrels 4½″. *Circa* 1840.

126 A Colt ·44 model 1860 Army percussion revolver with rare fluted cylinder. 14″, barrel 8″.

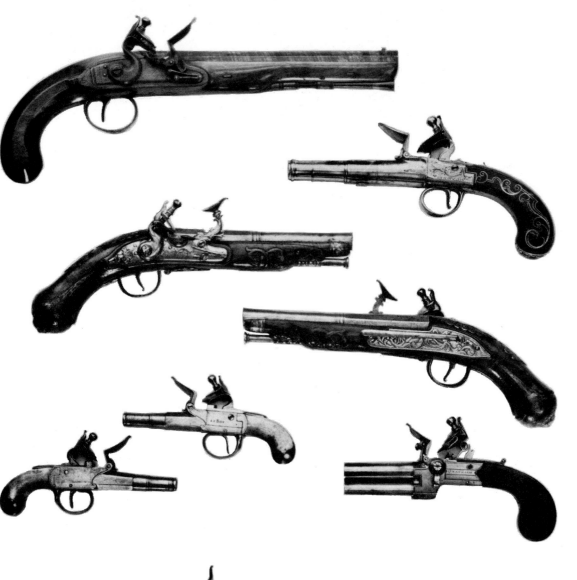

127   A flintlock duelling pistol by Sinkinson, Doncaster. 15″, barrel 9″. *Circa* 1800.

128   A cannon-barrelled flintlock boxlock overcoat pocket pistol by T. Pocock, Birmingham, with silver-wire inlaid butt. 10″, barrel 4″. *Circa* 1780.

129   A pair of Italian snaphaunce belt pistols. 11½″, barrels 7″. *Circa* 1700.

130   A pair of 'Segallas'-type all-steel flintlock boxlock pocket pistols by Le Roy. 6½″, barrels 2½″. *Circa* 1750.

131   A double-barrelled flintlock boxlock tap-action pocket pistol by J. & W. Richards, London. 8″, barrels 2½″. *Circa* 1800.

132   A pair of percussion double-barrelled turnover boxlock pocket pistols by Kavanagh, Dublin. 6″, barrels 1¾″. *Circa* 1830.

133   A pair of flintlock boxlock pocket pistols by Stacey, Sheffield. 6″, barrels 1½″. *Circa* 1800.

Flintlock, snaphaunce and percussion pistols.

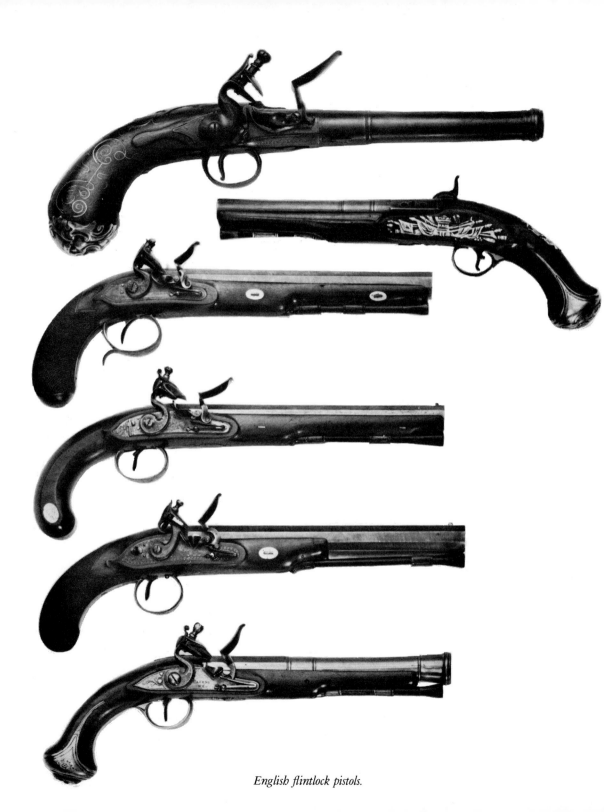

134 A Queen Anne silver-mounted flintlock pistol by Walker, London. 12½″, barrel 6″. *Circa* 1710.

136 A flintlock duelling pistol by Joseph Manton, London, with spurred trigger-guard. 14½″, barrel 10″. *Circa* 1810.

138 A flintlock duelling pistol by H. Nock, London, with rainproof flash-pan. 15¾″, barrel 10″. *Circa* 1810.

135 A silver-mounted percussion holster pistol by Brander, London, converted from flintlock. 14½″, barrel 8¼″. Originally *circa* 1750.

137 A flintlock duelling pistol by Gill & Knubley, London. 15″, barrel 9¾″. *Circa* 1800.

139 A brass-barrelled flintlock blunderbuss pistol by Cairn & Co. 15″, barrel 9″. Mid-eighteenth century.

English flintlock pistols.

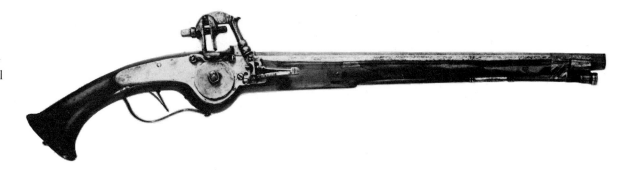

140 A Continental military wheel-lock pistol. *25″*, barrel 17½″. Mid-seventeenth century.

141 A Japanese matchlock pistol. 16½″, barrel 9½″. Nineteenth century.

142 A Spanish ripoll, Miquelet flintlock belt pistol, the stock with pierced and engraved brasswork. 15″, barrel 9″. Late seventeenth century.

143 A Brescian flintlock pistol. 19″, barrel 13″. Late seventeenth century.

Wheel-lock, matchlock and flintlock pistols.

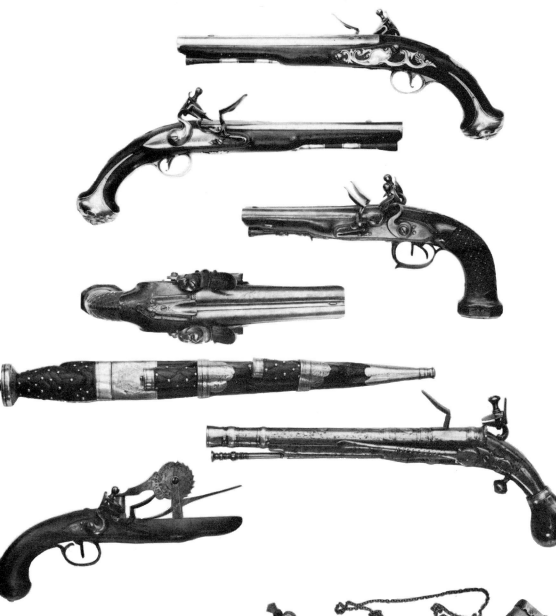

144   A pair of fully silver-mounted flintlock holster pistols by Barber, London, the mounts with London hallmark for 1765. 15", barrels 9".

145   A pair of French double-barrelled side-by-side flintlock holster pistols. 12", barrels 6¼". *Circa* 1780.

146   A Scottish dirk, blade 12", in its sheath with companion knife and fork. Late eighteenth century.

147   A Scottish Lowland flintlock pistol with heart butt. 14½", barrel 10½". Late seventeenth century.

148   A Continental upright flintlock eprouvette. 9½" overall. Mid-eighteenth century.

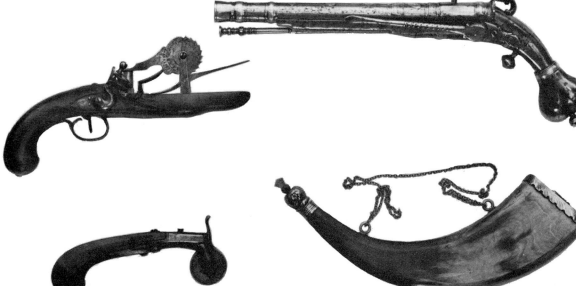

150   A Scottish powder flask. 12½" overall. Early nineteenth century.

149   An English hand-ignited eprouvette. 6" overall. Early eighteenth century.

Various eighteenth-century pistols, etc.

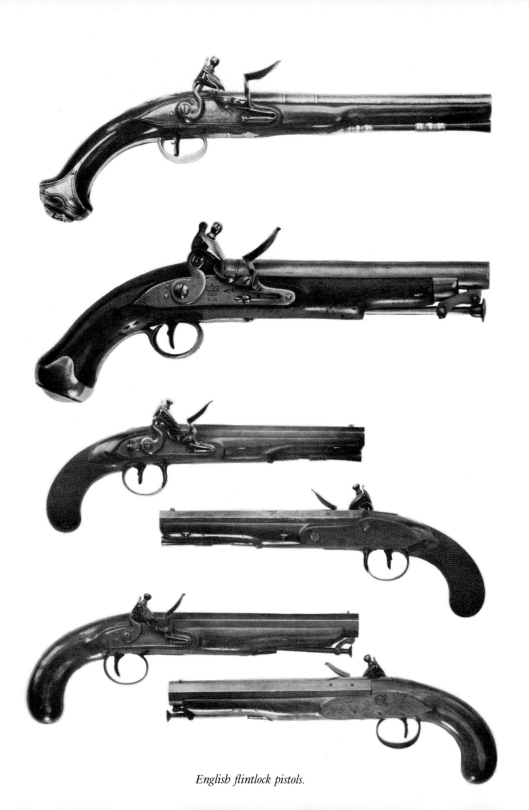

151 A fully silver-mounted flintlock holster pistol by J. Govers. 16½″, barrel 10″. Early eighteenth century.

152 A Tower new land pattern flintlock holster pistol, with swivel ramrod. 15″, barrel 9″. *Circa* 1800.

153 A pair of flintlock holster pistols by Barber & Boaler, Newark. 15″, barrels 8¾″. *Circa* 1800.

154 A pair of officer's flintlock holster pistols by H. Nock, London, with swivel ramrods. 15″, barrels 9¼″. *Circa* 1800.

English flintlock pistols.

155 A 6-shot 5-mm. pinfire 'Apache' pepperbox revolver-knuckleduster-dagger by L. Dolne. 8¼" open, blade 3". *Circa* 1880.

156 A harmonica pistol. 8", barrel 3½". *Circa* 1870.

157 A 4-barrelled duck's-foot mob pistol with flint-lock boxlock action, by Southall, London. 9", barrels 3". *Circa* 1800.

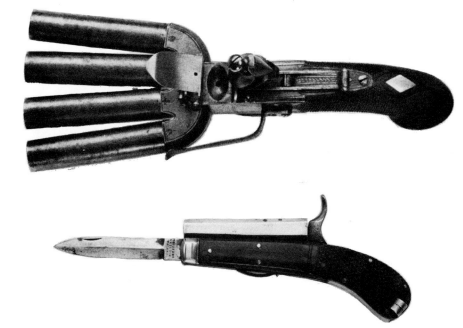

158 A ·28 percussion knife-pistol by Unwin & Rodgers. 6½" closed, barrel 3½", blade 3¾". *Circa* 1850.

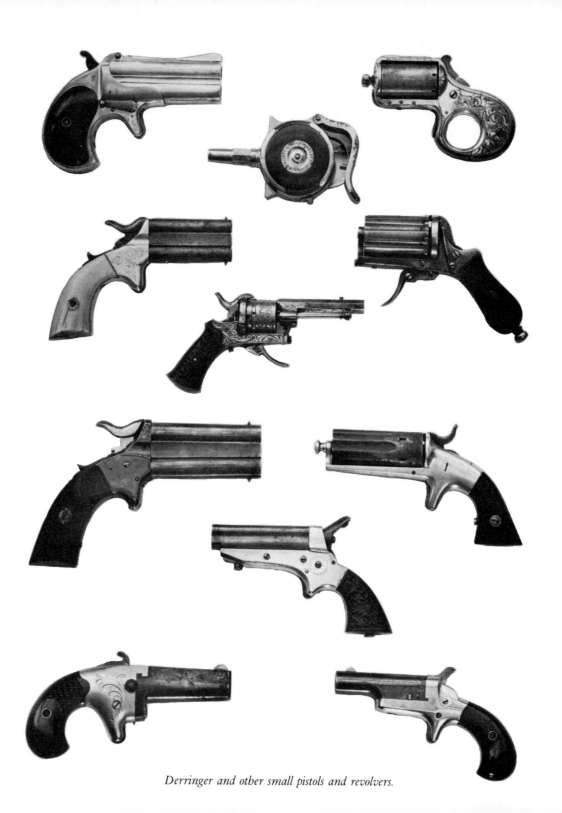

159 A Remington double-barrelled ·41 Derringer. 5″, barrels 3″. *Circa* 1880.

161 A 'Protector' palm pistol. 4″, barrel 1½″. *Circa* 1880.

162 A Woodward's patent 28 rimfire double-barrelled turnover pistol. 5″, barrels 2¼″. *Circa* 1870.

165 A Woodward's patent ·30 rimfire double-barrelled turnover pistol. 6¼″, barrels 3″. *Circa* 1870.

168 A Colt's patent ·41 rimfire No. 2 Derringer pistol. 5½″, barrel 2½″. *Circa* 1880.

160 A Reid 'My Friend' 7-shot ·22 rimfire knuckle-duster pepperbox revolver. 4½″, barrels 1½″. *Circa* 1870.

163 A pinfire pepperbox revolver. 4½″, barrels 1¾″. *Circa* 1870.

164 A small 5-mm. pinfire revolver. 5¼″, barrel 2¼″. *Circa* 1880.

166 A Bacon Arms Co. ·22 rimfire pepperbox revolver. 5¾″, barrels 2½″. *Circa* 1870.

167 A Sharp's patent ·22 rimfire 4-barrelled pepperbox pistol by Tipping & Lawden. 5″, barrels 2½″. *Circa* 1870.

169 A Colt's patent ·41 rimfire No. 3 Derringer pistol. 5″, barrel 2½″. *Circa* 1880.

Derringer and other small pistols and revolvers.

170 A brass-barrelled flintlock blunderbuss with top spring-bayonet, by Mewis & Co., London. 31″, barrel 15½″. Late eighteenth century.

171 A 6-shot revolving percussion pepperbox blunderbuss by Beckwith, London. 28½″, barrels 11½″. *Circa* 1840.

172 A Nock's patent 7-barrelled flintlock volley rifle by H. Nock, London. 36″, barrels 20″. *Circa* 1800.

173 An air gun by Beckwith, with sphere reservoir. 49½″, barrel 31″. Early nineteenth century.

Blunderbuss, rare multi-shot longarms and an air gun.

174 An Indian 4-shot revolving matchlock gun. 66″, barrel 41½″.

175 A German Landsknecht gun, the matchlock mechanism missing. 42″, barrel 30″. Early sixteenth century.

176 A small Indian flintlock blunderbuss. 18″, barrel 12″.

177 An Indian matchlock gun, Toradar, for a boy. 30″, barrel 21″.

178 An Afghan flintlock rifle with 'Sind' butt. 62″, barrel 46″.

Flintlocks and matchlocks.

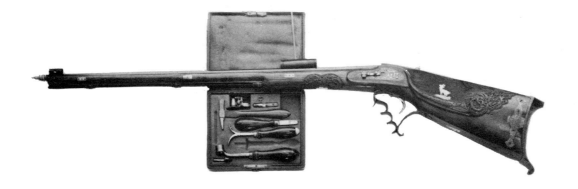

179 An Austrian breech-loading bellows air gun by P. Volkmann, Vienna, with case of accessories. 44½″, barrel 29½″.

180 A Kurdish Miquelet flintlock gun, with silver-inlaid stock. 45½″, barrel 32½″.

181 An Austrian flintlock rifle with oriental barrel. 48″, barrel 32″. Early eighteenth century.

182 An Austrian big-game percussion gun with oriental barrel. 58″, barrel 42½″. *Circa* 1830.

Austrian long guns and a Kurdish gun.

183 A Prince's patent percussion-capping breech-loading rifle. 39″, barrel 23″. *Circa* 1850.

184 A 6-shot 54-bore single-action percussion revolving rifle by J. Lang, London. 46″, barrel 28½″. *Circa* 1850.

185 A Winchester model 1866 brass-framed saddle carbine. 39″, barrel 20″.

186 A breech-loading falling-block harpoon gun by Alexander Henry. 51″, barrel 36″, with harpoon 49½″. *Circa* 1880.

187 An early harpoon gun with double flintlock mechanism. 35″, barrel 25″. Eighteenth century.

Interesting mid-nineteenth-century long guns and an early harpoon gun.

188 A double-barrelled 14-bore percussion big-game rifle by Isaac Hollis & Sons. 46″, barrels 30″. *Circa* 1850.

189 A 6-shot 11-mm. CF revolving rifle by Dreyse. 39″, barrel 20½″. *Circa* 1880.

190 A ·55 Sharp's patent breech-loading percussion carbine, dated 1852, with disc-primer ignition. 38″, barrel 21½″.

191 A Turkish Miquelet flintlock gun with six embossed silver barrel bands. 56″, barrel 42″.

192 A wheel-lock carbine, the inlaid stock bearing the Arms of Saxony. 32″, barrel 23″. Early seventeenth century.

193 A Balkan Miquelet flintlock gun with mother-of-pearl inlaid stock. 59″, barrel 45½″.

Various long guns.

194 A ·75 Tower 1839 pattern percussion musket, with its bayonet. *55″, barrel 39″.*

195 A 10-bore India pattern Brown Bess flintlock musket, bearing the 'Tower' and 'GR' markings, with its bayonet. *55″, barrel 39″. Circa 1810.*

196 A Dutch military matchlock musket. *55″, barrel 40″. Early seventeenth century.*

197 A single-barrelled flintlock sporting gun by John Manton & Son, Dover Street, London. *45½″, barrel 30″. Circa 1810.*

198 A Queen Anne cannon-barrelled flintlock carbine, with barrel link and skeleton butt, by H. Delaney, London. *37″, barrel 22″. Circa 1700.*

199 An English brass-barrelled military flintlock blunderbuss. *31½″, barrel 16″. Mid-eighteenth century.*

200 A double-barrelled 14-bore percussion sporting gun by Samuel & Charles Smith, London. *48″, barrels 32″. Circa 1850.*

Military and sporting long guns.

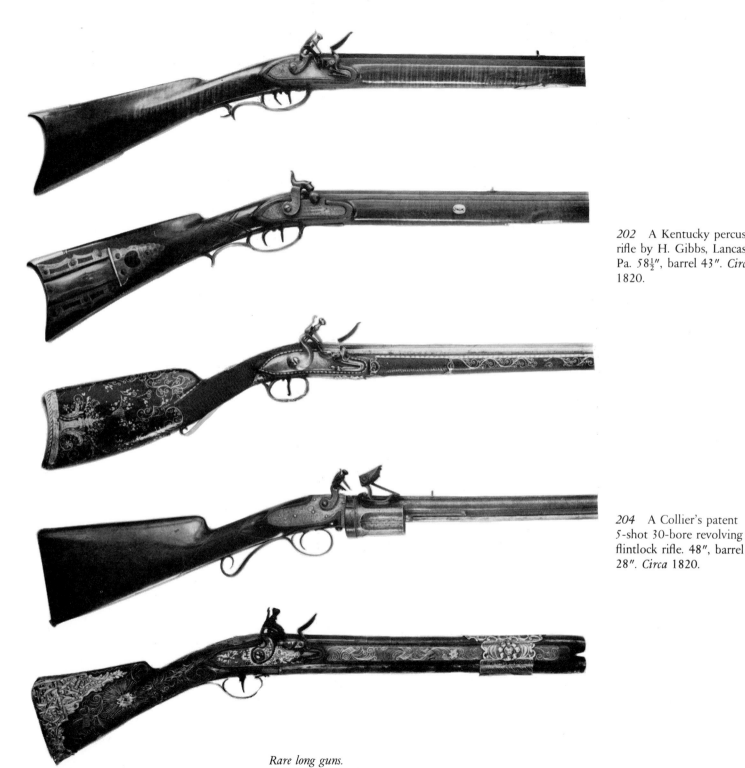

201 A Kentucky flintlock rifle by J. Thornton. 58", barrel 44". Late eighteenth century.

202 A Kentucky percussion rifle by H. Gibbs, Lancaster, Pa. 58½", barrel 43". *Circa* 1820.

203 A French silver-mounted flintlock gun with inlaid stock. 60½", barrel 45½".

204 A Collier's patent 5-shot 30-bore revolving flintlock rifle. 48", barrel 28". *Circa* 1820.

205 An Indian double-barrelled over-and-under flintlock carbine, with inlaid stock. 24½", barrels 13½".

Rare long guns.

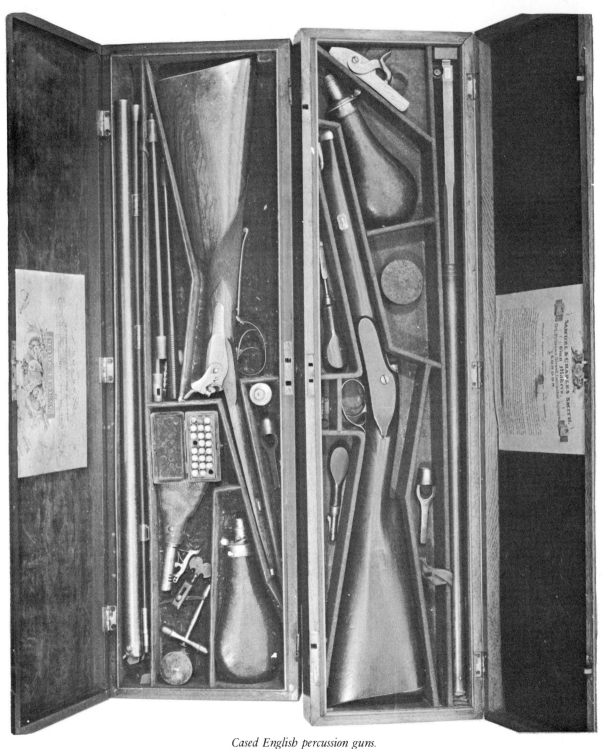

206 A double-barrelled 15-bore patchlock percussion sporting gun by Samuel Nock, Piccadilly, London. Cased with accessories, including a small case containing twenty spare strikers primed with caps. 42½", barrels 26½". *Circa* 1820.

207 A single-barrelled 14-bore Samuel & Charles Smith patent percussion sporting gun. Cased with accessories. 46", barrel 30". *Circa* 1840.

Cased English percussion guns.

208 (*extreme left*) A powder tester and adjustable powder measure. 7″. Seventeenth century.

209 (*left*) A powder measure. 5″. Seventeenth century.

213 (*left*) A North African Arab Miquelet flintlock. 7″.

215 (*extreme left*) An Indian powder flask in form of a fish, inlaid with ivory and mother-of-pearl. 9½″. Eighteenth century.

216 (*left*) An English silver-hilted small-sword, the hilt pierced with naval motifs. Blade 33″. Mid-eighteenth century.

210 (*centre*) A gunstock-shape copper pistol flask. 4½″. Mid-nineteenth century.

211 (*right*) An Italian steel powder flask. 8″. Seventeenth century.

212 (*centre*) A Scandinavian engraved ivory priming flask. 8″. Eighteenth century.

214 (*right*) A Baltic lock. 7″. Mid-seventeenth century.

217 (*centre*) Two Persian silver priming flasks. 7″ and 6½″.

218 (*right*) A Continental silver-hilted small-sword. Blade 32″. Mid-eighteenth century.

219 (*extreme right*) An Indian powder flask of enamelled brass. 8½″. Mid-eighteenth century.

AW—E

Powder flasks and measures, and detached lock mechanisms.

220 A pistol cleaning rod. 8″.

221 (*left*) A tin for Eley percussion caps.

222 (*right*) A tin of Tranter's patent lubricating grease.

223 An oil bottle.

224 (*extreme left*) A double-cavity bullet mould for an English percussion revolver. 7½″.

225 A turnscrew. 4½″.

226 (*centre*) A French pistol flask, 5″, with cross plunger charger.

227 (*right*) A nipple key. 4½″.

228 (*extreme right*) A pincer-type bullet mould. 5″.

229 (*extreme left*) Three-way leather-covered English pistol flask. 4¼″.

230 (*left*) Three-way copper English pistol flask. 4¼″.

231 (*right*) Embossed copper English pistol flask. 4¾″.

232 (*extreme right*) Bag-shaped copper English pistol flask for percussion revolver. 5″.

Powder flasks and accessories for use with pistols and revolvers, mostly mid-nineteenth century.

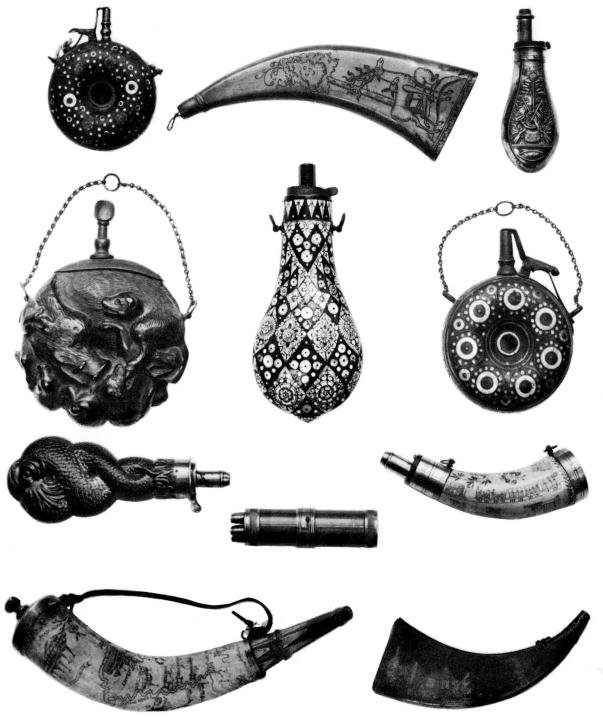

233 (top row, left) and 237 (second row, right) German powder flasks, circular, wood with staghorn inlay. 3½″ and 4″ diameter. Late seventeenth century.

234 (centre) Flattened horn powder flask, engraved with a stag. 9½″. Mid-eighteenth century.

235 (right) French copper pistol flask, embossed with hunting trophy. 5¼″. Mid-nineteenth century.

236 (left) German wooden powder flask, carved with boar-hunting scene. 5″ diameter. Seventeenth century.

238 (centre) Indian powder flask, inlaid with horn, ivory and mother-of-pearl. 7½″. Eighteenth or nineteenth century.

239 (left) An English embossed copper powder flask of the rare 'entwined dolphins' pattern. 8″. Mid-nineteenth century.

240 (centre) A Colt Paterson multiple powder flask. 5½″. Circa 1840.

241 (right) An English powder horn, engraved with an early railway train. 8″. Mid-nineteenth century.

242 (left) An American 'map' engraved powder horn, dated 1758. 14″.

243 (right) A Scottish powder horn. 11″. Seventeenth century.

Powder flasks.

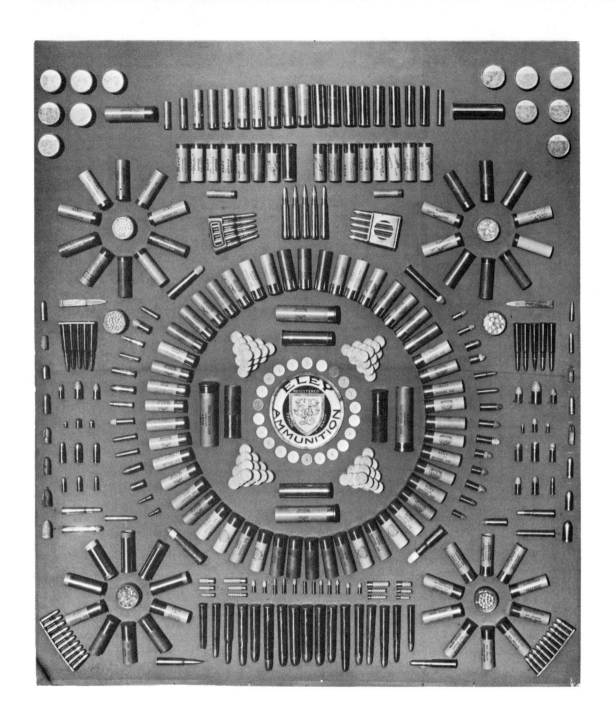

244 An Eley cartridge display of sporting and military ammunition. *45″×42″*.

Swords & Daggers, European

Anelace   A civilian short sword generally associated with the baselard (*q.v.*) type seen in English church brasses of the fourteenth and fifteenth centuries.

Backsword   A sword with a single-edged blade, the back edge being flat. Often found with basket hilts (*289–91*).

Badelaire   A sixteenth-century short sword or hanger with broad blade and recurved (*q.v.*) cross-guard.

Baldric   A shoulder belt from which the sword was suspended.

Ballock-knife   See *Kidney Dagger*.

Band Sword   A short sword, or sidearm, worn by bandsmen. The hilt was often entirely of brass. A well-known pattern was the Victorian issue with 'gothic' hilt.

Baselard   A dagger, or short sword, of fourteenth- and fifteenth-century date. The hilt was similar in form to a capital letter I. The length of the blade varied.

Basket-hilt   A term used to describe the hilt of a sword which completely covers the hand. It is generally of barred openwork design. The hilt of the Scottish broadsword is a well-known example (*289–93*).

Bastard Sword   Another term for the 'hand-and-a-half' sword. It had a long grip, allowing the user to employ both hands. The grip was not as long as on the two-handed sword.

Bilbo   A term generally given to the Spanish military cup-hilted swords of the eighteenth century. They often have double-edged blades bearing a date, etc.

Bowie Knife   A term given to a general-purpose hunting or fighting knife, usually with broad, single-edged blade having a clipped back point (i.e. a slightly cut-away back edge for about 2 inches from the tip).

The origin was the knife made in 1830 by an Arkansas blacksmith to the design and order of the legendary James Bowie, a colonel in the Texas Army, who commanded the forces at the Alamo. The early Bowie knives sometimes had a brass strip along the back edge of the blade.

In the American West the conditions during the middle and late nineteenth century made necessary the carrying of a knife for protection, and it became more popular as the feats of James Bowie with his knife were published abroad.

American knives were made based on the Bowie design and soon afterwards the English cutlers started manufacture. Two famous makers were Wostenholm and Rodgers of Sheffield. Many varieties were produced, usually with German-silver mounts, the grips also of German silver, wood, horn or ivory.

The blades of the English-made knives often had etched mottoes such as 'Death to Traitors', 'United States, Home of the Brave', etc.

Smaller knives with double-edged blades, folding knives with clipped-back blades, and others, are often included in the term 'Bowie knife' (*298–301, 401*).

Broadsword   A sword with straight broad double-edged blade. A well-known example is the Scottish Broadsword (*q.v.*) (*275, 277*).

Chape   The mount at the tip end of a sword scabbard or dagger sheath. Usually of metal and decorated *en suite* with the locket (*q.v.*).

Cinquedea   An Italian late fifteenth- or early sixteenth-century dagger with tapering double-edged blade. The name derived from the fact that the blade was some five fingers' width at the hilt, and it was often fluted and engraved. Some Cinquedea were virtually small swords.

Claymore   The Scottish two-handed sword used in the fifteenth and sixteenth centuries. The down-drooping quillons had pierced trefoil or quatrefoil terminals. The name 'claymore' is often erroneously given to the more recent basket-hilted broadsword.

Colichemarde   A type of blade found on small-swords. It is broad at the forte, for about a third of its length, and then tapers suddenly with 'shoulders' to a narrower form for the remaining part. The name derives from Otto von Königsmark, a Swedish Count.

Court Sword   A light dress sword generally of small-sword type. It was first worn in the late seventeenth century and is still worn today. The modern version has a simple cut-steel hilt.

Couteau-de-chasse   The French term for a hunting sword or hanger.

Cruciform Hilt   A sword or dagger with plain crosspiece at right angles to the hilt, thus forming a cross. A form much used during the medieval period and more recently on the Sudanese national sword.

Cup Hilt   A type of rapier hilt in which the hand is guarded by a metal cup below the quillons. It is frequently found on Spanish rapiers, and was often finely pierced and chased (*286*).

Cutlass   A term generally given to the short sword with broad, single-edged, curved blade, used by sailors. The semi-basket hilt is often of plain iron.

Dague à Rouelles   Alternatively *Rondel Dagger*. A fourteenth- to early sixteenth-century dagger, the hilt having disc pommel and guards, and slender blade.

Dirk   A term given to: (*a*) a Scottish dagger derived from the kidney dagger, (*b*) a naval dagger and (*c*) sometimes applied to a Japanese dagger. The Scottish dirk has retained the same form for over two hundred years. The more recent type used for Highland dress, or military dress wear, has a sheath with sockets for companion knife and fork. The mounts are often of silver or gilt, and the pommels inset with cut cairngorm stones (*303, 308*).

Eared Dagger   A form of fifteenth- and sixteenth-century dagger derived from an oriental type, the hilt having a pommel of double 'eared' form. The Turkish yataghan has a similar hilt, often of walrus ivory or horn.

Estoc or **Tuck**   A thrusting sword, of the fifteenth to early seventeenth centuries, with long stiff slender blade of square or triangular section.

Executioner's Sword   A broad-bladed sword with cruciform hilt used on the Continent through several centuries. The blade often bears inscriptions and scenes relating to its use (*265, 267*).

Falchion   A short sword with curved single-edged blade, current from the middle ages to the seventeenth century.

Flamberge   A rapier with simplified hilt and long slender blade, introduced about 1600. The hilt had short straight quillons and only a shallow saucer-shaped guard. It was not fitted with knuckle-bow or *pas d'âne* (*q.v.*). This form shows a step in the transition from rapier to small-sword.

Flamboyant Blade   A blade of serpentine or wavy form. It is often seen on the Malay kris and much less frequently on European swords and daggers (*357*).

Foible   The part of a sword blade nearest the point.

Foil   A slender-bladed sword for thrusting, used in fencing. The hilt has a dish guard or double-loop of figure-eight form.

Forte   The part of a blade nearest to the hilt.

Frog   A leather or cloth attachment to the belt for carrying a sword or bayonet.

Fuller   The groove(s) in a sword blade.

Grip   The part of a sword or dagger hilt that is held in the hand. Grips are made of various materials such as horn, ivory, wood, etc., and may be elaborately bound with plaited wire. See *Rapier, Small-sword.*

Guard   The part of a sword hilt which protects the hand. See *Rapier, Small-sword.*

Hand-and-a-half Sword   See *Bastard Sword.*

Hanger   A short sword with slightly curved single-edged blade. It was often used by horsemen and also by Naval Officers.

Hilt   See illustration.

Holbein Dagger   A sixteenth-century dagger evolved from the baselard, also known as Swiss dagger. The hilt was I-shaped and the double-edged blade was short and leaf-shaped. This form was reintroduced in Nazi Germany in the regulation SS and SA daggers.

Hunting Sword   A short sword, often with curved blade, used by huntsmen through several centuries. The hilt is frequently of staghorn, or ivory, with silver or brass mounts which may have designs of animals' heads or hoofs thereon (*294, 297*). Sometimes a pistol was fitted in the hilt (*283*).

Kidney Dagger   A term for the type of dagger with a pair of rounded lobes instead of quillons, formerly known as a ballock knife. It was used in north-western Europe from the fourteenth to seventeenth centuries.

Knuckle-guard or **Knuckle-bow**   A curved bar or plate on a sword hilt which protects the knuckles. See *Rapier, Small-sword.*

Landsknecht Dagger   A type of dagger worn by the German Landsknechts, a corps of foot mercenaries, raised by the Emperor Maximilian in the first half of the sixteenth century. The hilt has a grip tapering towards the quillons. The sheath has bands of raised decoration suggestive of the puffed and slashed costume of the Landsknechts.

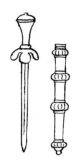

Landsknecht Sword   A sword used by the Landsknechts, with distinctive quillons of horizontal recurved S form, often like a figure 8 (*266, 276*).

Langets   Metal strips fitted on the hafts of staff weapons for protection and strength. A term also applied to the two small lugs projecting down from a sword hilt on which there is often a badge or motif.

Left-hand Dagger   A sixteenth- and seventeenth-century dagger, usually used together with a rapier. The common form had a cruciform hilt, with straight or down-curved quillons, and a single side ring or shell guard (*307*). See also *Main Gauche.*

Lloyd's Presentation Swords   Between 1803 and 1809 a fine series of presentation naval swords were given by the Patriotic Fund at Lloyd's to officers who distinguished themselves in action. Four grades were made: £30, £50, £100 and Trafalgar, the last a variation of the £100 design. These swords were richly decorated and had broad curved blades bearing details of the action (*255*).

Locket   The top mount of a sword scabbard or dagger sheath including the mouth portion where the blade enters. It sometimes bears the maker's name.

Main Gauche A seventeenth-century left-hand dagger (*q.v.*) used in conjunction with a rapier as a parrying weapon. The Spanish form had a broad triangular guard and long straight quillons (*264*).

Mameluke Hilt A pattern of hilt found on generals' swords, levée swords, etc. It was based on the form of the Turkish sabre hilt and had a pistol-butt shaped grip, often of ivory, and a gilt brass crosspiece.

Military Swords From the late eighteenth century, regulation-pattern swords were worn by British and other soldiers. Some commonly encountered are the 1796 pattern sabre with steel stirrup hilt (*q.v.*) (*251*); the Georgian infantry officer's sword with gilt brass hilt, having double oval shell guard and silver-wire grip; the 1822 infantry officer's sword with brass semi-basket hilt bearing the royal cypher; the 1895 pattern infantry officer's sword with plated semi-basket hilt incorporating the royal cypher (*248*). Various other patterns were carried by Cavalry, Scottish regiments, Artillery, and so on. Short swords, or side-arms, were worn by bandsmen, pioneers, etc. These latter usually had all-brass hilts (*252–4*).

Misericord A narrow-bladed, sharp-pointed dagger, made to penetrate the joints or vizor of plate armour and give the *coup de grâce* to a fallen adversary.

Mortuary Sword An English Civil War period basket-hilted sword. The heart-shaped guard often bears a design of human busts, thought to represent Charles I.

Mourning Sword A small-sword with simple hilt of plain blackened steel.

Naval Swords In the eighteenth century British naval officers used various types of sword, i.e. hangers, small-swords, spadroons. By the early nineteenth century regulation-pattern swords were worn (*255–9*). A distinctive feature of naval officers' swords and dirks for over a century has been a gilt brass hilt with lion's-head pommel and fishskin grip (*246*).

Pappenheimer A rapier with swept hilt having pierced double-shell guards. The name derives from Marshal Maximilian Pappenheim. Also referred to as a 'Walloon Sword' (*280*).

Pas d'Âne The two ring guards projecting downwards from the quillons on a sword hilt, and serving the purpose of protecting the thumb and forefinger. As the small-sword developed, the *pas d'âne* became smaller, then merely ornamental and finally disappeared at the end of the eighteenth century. See *Rapier, Small-sword*.

Pillow Sword A mid-seventeenth-century sword with simple hilt having a small cross guard and sometimes one side-ring. The blade is usually slender and double-edged.

Pipe-back Blade A form of blade of German origin found on naval and military swords of the second quarter of the nineteenth century. The back edge had a rounded pipe-like spine.

Poignard or **Poniard** A small dagger with slender blade, used for stabbing.

Pommel The knob on the end of the hilt of a sword, or dagger. Sometimes the term is also used to describe a pistol butt. See *Rapier, Small-sword*.

Quillon The extended crosspiece of the hilt of a sword or a dagger, usually straight, but sometimes curved. See *Rapier, Small-sword*.

Quillon Dagger   A general term given to a dagger with a cruciform hilt (*q.v.*) (*305*).

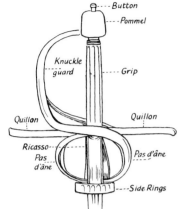

Rapier   A long straight-bladed sword of the sixteenth and seventeenth centuries. Originally used for cut-and-thrust play, it gradually developed into a thrusting weapon only. It subsequently evolved into the small-sword in the late seventeenth century. Rapier hilts were usually quite elaborate and two distinct patterns were the cup hilt and swept hilt (*q.v.*) (*282, 284–8*).

Recurved   A term used to describe a blade or cross-guard which curves one way and then another (similar to an open S).

Ricasso   The flat oblong part of a sword blade nearest to the hilt and before the actual cutting edge. See *Rapier, Small-sword*.

Rondel Dagger   See *Dague à Rouelles*.

Sabre   A sword with curved, single-edged, blade, generally a cavalry weapon (*273, 274*).

Saw-back Blade   The British Pioneer sword of 1856–1903, also certain bayonets, hunting swords, etc., had a saw-back edge to the blade. Some Indian swords also had wicked-looking blades with serrated edges.

Scabbard   The sheath of a sword or bayonet.

Schiavona   The Venetian broadsword of the seventeenth and eighteenth centuries. It had a distinctive basket-hilt with barred and trellised openwork design (*278, 281*).

Schleger   The duelling sabre used by German students in the nineteenth and early twentieth centuries. It has a large basket-hilt with coloured felt lining and straight blade, having only about 2 inches of edge sharp at the blunt-tipped end.

Scimitar   A sword with curved, single-edged blade originating in the East. It often has a 'Mameluke' or 'pistol-shaped' hilt. See Shamshir (*under* Oriental Weapons).

Scottish Broadsword   The distinctive basket-hilted sword with broad double-edged blade, carried by the Scots since the seventeenth century. The type survives in the regulation pattern of the Highland regiments. Designs of hearts and S motifs are frequently used on the hilts (*277, 292, 293*).

Shell Guard   The oval, heart- or shell-shaped guard on a sword, usually mounted at right angles to the blade at the base of the hilt.

Sidearm   A short sword worn by bandsmen, pioneers, artillerymen, police, or prison warders (*252, 254*).

Sinclairsabel   The term given to a late sixteenth-century sword used in Scandinavia. They were imported from Germany and had a long flat curved blade. The hilt consisted of a triangular guard with spatulate recurved quillons, and additional rings.

Skean Dhu   A small Scottish knife, carried in the stocking for dress use. Often silver-mounted, the grip carved with strapwork and having a cairngorm stone pommel.

Small-sword   The successor of the rapier worn in the late seventeenth and through the eighteenth centuries. It was both a civilian and military weapon. The hilt usually had a double shell guard, short quillons, knuckle-bow and spherical pommel. Many hilts were elaborate and were finely pierced or chiselled in silver, gilt metal or steel. The blade was frequently of slender triangular section and often of colichemarde type (*q.v.*). See also *Court Sword* (*271, 272*).

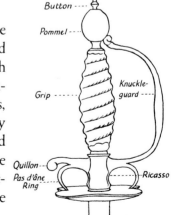

Society Sword   A dress sword worn by members of a veteran's society, masonic institution, etc. The hilts are usually cruciform, sometimes elaborate, and bearing symbols. The blades are frequently etched with the name of the society or wearer, symbols, or other such inscriptions (*383*).

Spadroon   A light 'cut and thrust' sword. The name given to the British infantry officer's sword of the late eighteenth century.

Stiletto   A small seventeenth-century dagger with slender stabbing blade, the hilt and crosspiece often entirely of steel (*366*). Some were carried by gunners and these had a scale marked on the blade (*263*).

Stirrup Hilt   A form of hilt, usually on military swords, having a single knuckle bow somewhat similar in form to a stirrup (*251*).

Swept Hilt   A form of rapier hilt with barred and looped guard, the knuckle-bow(s) sweeping down to join the crossguard (*288*).

Tang   The narrow rectangular part of a sword blade on which the hilt is mounted. It continues right up to the pommel button, at which point it is riveted down to hold the hilt components secure.

Trousse-de-chasse   A set of implements, usually a large knife and sundry small knives, etc., contained in one sheath. It was used when hunting to eviscerate the kill (*364*).

Two-handed Sword   A large sword which requires the use of both hands to wield it. The grip is elongated accordingly. Swords of this type were carried in Europe for fighting and parade use, and various forms of two-handed swords from the Orient are encountered.

Walloon Sword   Another name given to the Pappenheimer (*q.v.*).

Wolf Mark   The 'running wolf' symbol found on sword blades was the makers' mark of Solingen and Passau in Germany. Many of these fine blades were made and exported to numerous countries.

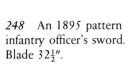

245 A 1908 pattern cavalry officer's sword. Blade 35″.

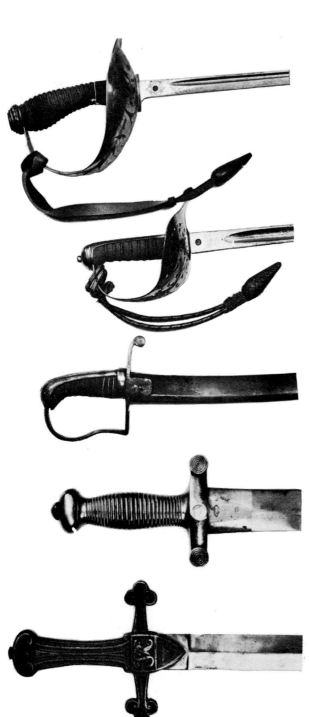

248 An 1895 pattern infantry officer's sword. Blade 32½″.

251 A 1796 pattern Light Cavalry sabre. Blade 33″.

252 A French 'Roman'-type artillery sidearm with all-brass hilt. Blade 19″.

254 A Victorian band sword with Gothic hilt. Blade 18″.

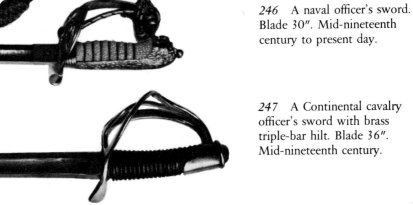

246 A naval officer's sword. Blade 30″. Mid-nineteenth century to present day.

247 A Continental cavalry officer's sword with brass triple-bar hilt. Blade 36″. Mid-nineteenth century.

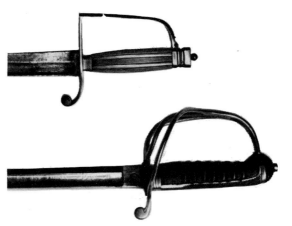

249 A British officer's sword. Blade 32″. Late eighteenth century.

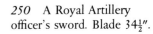

250 A Royal Artillery officer's sword. Blade 34½″.

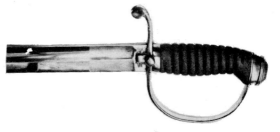

253 A British Victorian police or prison warder's sword. Blade 24″.

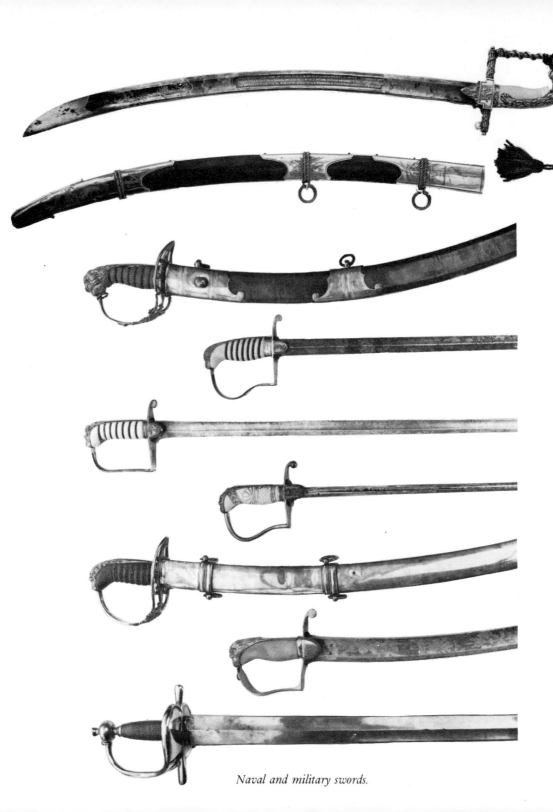

255 A Lloyd's Patriotic Fund 30-guinea presentation sword. Blade 30″. *Circa* 1805.

256 An 1803 pattern general officer's sword. Blade 30″.

257 A Georgian naval officer's sword. Blade 28½″. *Circa 1815.*

258 A Georgian naval officer's sword. Blade 32½″. *Circa 1805.*

259 A Georgian naval midshipman's sword. Blade 26″.

260 A British general officer's sword, 1803 pattern, bearing the crest of the Honourable East India Company. Blade 30″.

261 A Georgian sabre of a type used by British naval officers for fighting. Blade 30″. *Circa 1800.*

262 A Swedish 1729 pattern cavalry trooper's sword. Blade 39″.

Naval and military swords.

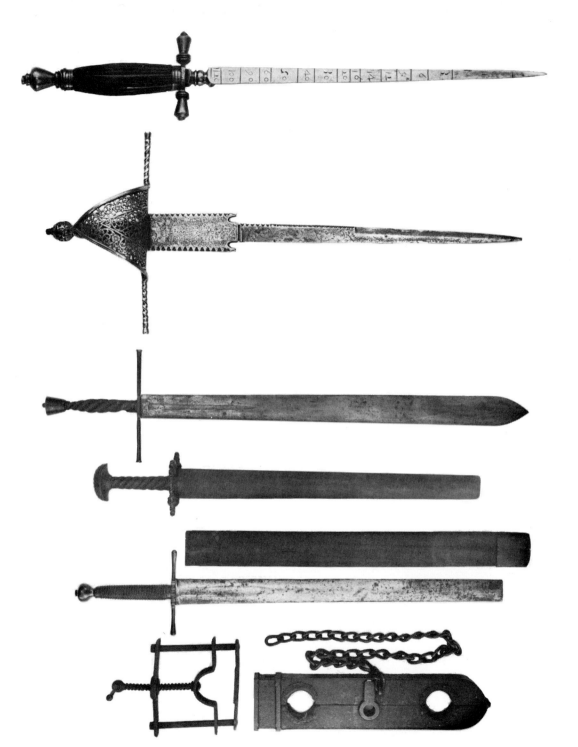

263 An Italian gunner's stiletto. Blade 9½". Mid-seventeenth century.

264 A Spanish *main gauche* dagger. Blade 19¼". Mid-seventeenth century.

265 An executioner's sword from Augsburg. Blade 36"×3" (at widest). Late sixteenth century.

266 A Landsknecht sword. Blade 28"×2½" wide. Early sixteenth century.

267 An executioner's sword from Augsburg. Blade 31"×2½" wide. Late sixteenth century.

268 A foot-screw torture implement from Nuremberg Castle.

269 A hand pillory from Nuremberg Castle. 22".

European swords and daggers.

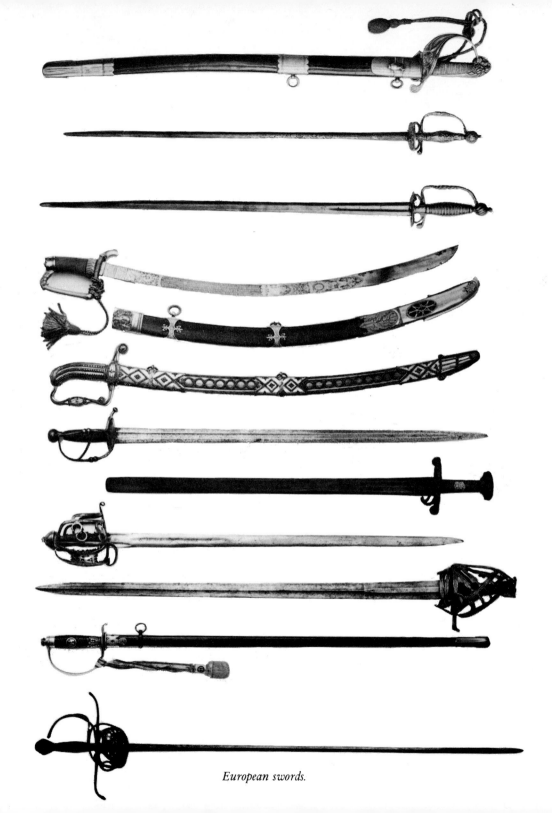

270 An early Victorian British naval officer's sword. Blade 31″.

271 A Continental silver-hilted small-sword. Blade 29½″. Mid-eighteenth century.

272 An English silver-hilted small-sword. Blade 32″. Mid-eighteenth century.

273 A presentation Georgian military sabre. Blade 31½″.

274 A Georgian military sabre with cut steel and beaded hilt and scabbard. Blade 31″.

275 A German military broadsword. Blade 33″. Late seventeenth century.

276 A Landsknecht sword. Blade 28½″. Early sixteenth century.

277 A Scottish basket-hilted broadsword. Blade 31″. Early eighteenth century.

278 A Venetian schiavona. Blade 36″. Early eighteenth century.

279 A Nazi SS officer's sword. Blade 33″.

280 A Pappenheimer rapier. Blade 37½″.

European swords.

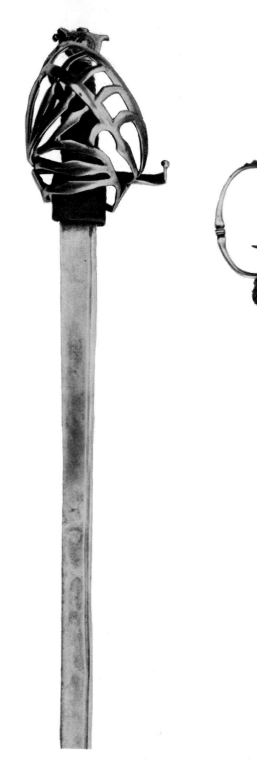

281 A Venetian schiavona.
Blade 35″. Eighteenth
century.

283 A combined hunting
sword and flintlock pistol.
Blade 26½″. Mid-eighteenth
century.

282 A Spanish barred-hilt
rapier. Blade 44½″. Early
seventeenth century.

European swords.

284 (*extreme left*) A German rapier with five-barred hilt and double shell guard. Blade 44″. Late sixteenth century.

285 (*left*) A Spanish rapier with swept hilt. Blade 47″. Late sixteenth century.

286 (*centre*) An Italian rapier with pierced cup hilt. Blade 46″. Mid-seventeenth century.

287 (*right*) An English rapier with dish guard. Blade 36″. Mid-seventeenth century.

288 (*extreme right*) A German rapier with swept hilt. Blade 41½″. Late sixteenth century.

289 (*extreme left*) A Scottish backsword with trellised basket hilt and bun pommel. Blade 32½″. Mid-eighteenth century.

290 (*left*) A similar back-sword. Blade 38½″.

291 (*centre*) A presentation Scottish backsword, dated 1812. Blade 33″.

292 (*right*) A Scottish broadsword. Blade 34″. Mid-eighteenth century.

293 (*extreme right*) A Scottish broadsword. Blade 33″. Late eighteenth century.

Scottish and European swords.

294 (extreme left)   An
English hunting sword, brass
hilt with staghorn grip,
maker's mark on blade.
Blade 22″. Late seventeenth
century.

295 (left)   A French hunting
sword, gilt all-brass hilt with
rocaille designs. Blade 20½″.
Mid-eighteenth century.

296 (right)   German hunting
sword, brass hilt chased with
a hunting scene; ivory grips.
Blade 23½″. Late eighteenth
century.

297 (extreme right)   South
American hunting sword
with bird's-head pommel.
Blade 22″. Mid-nineteenth
century.

Hunting swords.

298 and 299 Two Victorian
Sheffield-made Bowie knives
with etched blades. Blades
7″ and 8″.

300 A Victorian hunting
knife by Unwin & Rodgers,
Sheffield, 1862. Blade 12″.

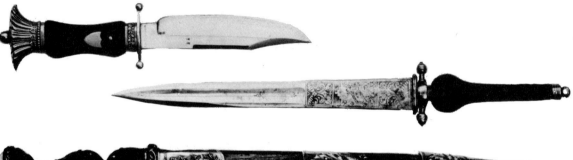

301 A Victorian Bowie
knife with 'clipped-back'
blade. Blade 6½″.

302 A plug bayonet. Blade
11¼″. Early eighteenth
century.

303 A Victorian Scottish
military dirk. Blade 12″.

304 (extreme left) A French silver-hilted hunting dirk with sheath. Blade 11″. *Circa* 1803. (Formerly in the J. D. Aylward Collection.)

305 (left) A quillon dagger. Blade 14½″. *Circa* 1300.

306 (centre) An Italian all-steel stiletto. Blade 8″. Mid-seventeenth century.

308 (right) A Scottish dirk. Blade 14″. Mid-eighteenth century.

307 (extreme right) A left-hand dagger, with counter-guard. Blade 12½″. Late sixteenth century.

309 (right) A Victorian silver-mounted dagger and sheath. Blade 4″.

Various daggers, dirks, etc.

Sundry Weapons

POLEARMS OR STAFF WEAPONS, MACES, CROSSBOWS, FLAILS, ETC.

Arbalest   The crossbow used in medieval Europe. Frequently the stocks were finely inlaid with engraved staghorn. Some were spanned by hand, but the heavier types were drawn by windlass, cranequin (*q.v.*) or goat's-foot lever (*313, 316*).

Arrow   The projectile shot from a bow (*q.v.*). It has been used from the earliest times and by many races. The head usually has a pointed metal tip, sometimes barbed. Some ancient races and the North American Indian tribes used flint or stone arrow heads.

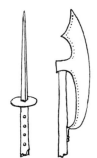

Awl-pike   A staff weapon with long spiked blade, fitted with a disc at the base. It was used for thrusting.

Axe   A weapon and implement used through the ages, having a head with sharp edge mounted on a haft. The earliest type had stone heads, then bronze, and later iron. Many races used the axe. Those of European origin are generally heavier than the oriental types, which are often elaborately engraved and overlaid.

Bardiche   A polearm with long, slender, curved axe blade, often crescent-shaped.

Bayonet   An edged weapon for attachment to the muzzle end of a firearm to convert it into a pike. The earliest form was the plug bayonet with a tapered grip which fitted into the muzzle. It could also be separately used as a short sword or dagger. Later bayonets had a ring or socket which fitted over the muzzle, or were attached at the

side on a lug. Some were also fitted with a hilt for use as a sword (*302, 379, 382*).

Bill   A long polearm with a hooked blade having spikes on the back and tip. Its origin was as an agricultural implement and several varieties of staff weapons were developed from it.

Boar Spear   A stout weapon for the hunt. It had a wide leaf-shaped blade with central strengthening ridge and often a small crosspiece or toggle. It was sometimes carried by Landsknecht officers in the sixteenth century.

Bolt   The short projectile arrow shot from the crossbow. The steel tip was usually of square section, either pointed or blunt. Some had flights of wood or leather. Also known as a quarrel.

Bow   The oldest form of projectile weapon used by many races through the ages. It is basically a long thin strip of springy wood with a cord stretched between the two ends, the tension pulling the wood into a slight arc. See *Arrow*.

Buckler   A shield for parrying blows, generally small and circular in shape. It had a handle on the reverse and was held in the left hand.

Calthrop   A spiked implement, numbers of which were placed on the ground to deter advancing cavalry or troops.

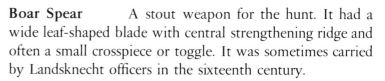

Catch Pole   An implement used to catch an enemy or villain, by the neck. It consisted of a pole with a forked head from which he could not escape, once trapped.

Celt   An ancient axe head of stone or bronze.

Combination Weapon   A weapon in which two or more weapons were combined, e.g. sword-pistols or axe-pistols. Many varieties exist, including some ingenious Indian-made pieces. Axes and maces from India frequently have a dagger which screws into the haft.

Cranequin   A crank-operated rack-and-pinion implement used to span the crossbow.

Crossbow   See *Arbalest*; also *Bolt, Cranequin, Goat's-foot Lever,* and *Prodd* (*313, 314, 316*).

Flail   A haft with a shorter spiked haft or ball attached by a chain. It could be a polearm, or a hand weapon for mounted use.

> **Glaive**   A staff weapon with curved knife-like blade. Used in medieval Europe and more recently in China.
>
> **Goat's-foot Lever**   A forked lever used to span the lighter form of crossbow.
>
> **Halberd**   A polearm with an axe-head usually backed by a pointed fluke, and with a vertical spiked blade as a continuation of the haft. Used from the thirteenth century as a fighting weapon, it later became more ornamental for parade use. British Army sergeants carried a halberd in the eighteenth century (*312*).
>
> **Holy-water Sprinkler**   A hafted weapon with spiked head. Specimens are known with hand-ignited pistol barrels in the head.

Lance   One of the oldest weapons in the world. Basically a straight shaft with a pointed metal tip, often leaf-shaped. Much used by cavalry through the ages.

Linstock   A polearm of pike form with two serpentine holders below the spike to hold lighted matches for igniting cannon.

Lochaber Axe   A Scottish polearm, with elongated, single-edged blade, usually having a hook at the top end.

Long Bow   See *Bow.*

Mace   A hand weapon, often entirely of steel, with a spiked or flanged head (*310*).

Morning Star   A flail with spherical spiked head attached to the haft by means of a chain; also an infantry weapon of peasant origin comprising a long wooden club with spikes on the head (*Morgenstern*).

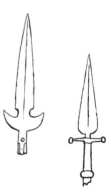

> **Partizan**   A staff weapon with wide spear-shaped blade, often having upward-curved projections at either side of the base. Many were made for ceremonial use and bore coats of arms.
>
> **Pike**   A long spear-type polearm about 18 feet long with small leaf-shaped head, used by the infantry against cavalry.
>
> **Plug Bayonet**   See *Bayonet.*

Pole Axe   A staff weapon with axe-head having a hammer, or spike at rear.

Prodd   A crossbow designed to shoot stones or bullets, instead of quarrels. It had a double bow-string with small central pouch to hold the projectile. Also known as a Stone Bow. Late examples were made into the early nineteenth century in England, and were used for sporting purposes (*314*).

Quarrel   See *Bolt.*

Quiver   A container for carrying arrows, worn on the belt or on a shoulder strap.

Sling   A simple projectile weapon used from ancient times. It consists of a strip of leather or other material, with a central pouch to hold the stone.

Socket Bayonet   A bayonet, generally with a triangular blade, that was affixed to the musket by a tubular section which fitted over the muzzle. This type of bayonet was used with the British 'Brown Bess' and later longarms.

Spontoon   A polearm of pike type with leaf-shaped blade, usually with crosspiece. It was used as a military weapon and was carried by English sergeants as late as 1830.

Stone Bow   See *Prodd.*

Sword Bayonet   A bayonet with a hand grip for alternative use as a sword. Some had a simple crosspiece with ring for the barrel, others had a knuckle guard (*379*).

Sword Breaker   A dagger-type weapon with serrated blade designed to catch the opponent's sword blade and snap it; also the notches or recesses at the base of the blades of many seventeenth-century left-hand daggers.

Sword Stick   A walking stick in which a sword blade is concealed. The handle of the stick acts as the hilt and often a press-button release is fitted. In recent times blades have been fitted in officers' batons and umbrellas.

Targe   The Scottish circular shield. It was of wood covered with leather and studded with patterns of brass nails and bosses.

Voulge   A French term applied to the original Swiss form of thirteenth-century halberd which continued to be used later alongside the more fully developed weapon.

310 A German war mace, all steel with six-flanged head. 20″. Late fifteenth century.

311 A Runka polearm. Blade 24½″. Mid-sixteenth century.

312 A halberd. Blade 24″. Mid-sixteenth century.

Polearms.

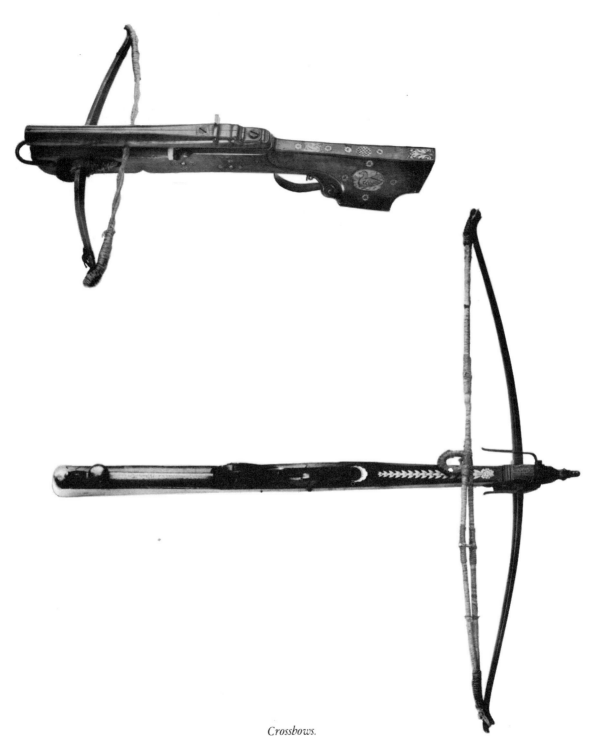

313 A German crossbow. 20½″, span 15″. Sixteenth century.

314 A stone bow, or prodd, by Richardson, Manchester. Span 28″. Late eighteenth century.

Crossbows.

316 A stirrup crossbow with windlass. 42″, span 29″. Sixteenth century.

315 A Chinese repeating crossbow with box magazine on top. 35″, span 29″.

Crossbows.

Eastern & Native Weapons

Ancus   The Indian elephant goad. It has a pointed tip and a curved spike on the side. Most examples seen average about 20 inches overall, and some are very ornamental (*390*).

Assegai   A spear used by the native tribes of South Africa. It usually has an iron leaf-shaped head.

Axe   A weapon used in many countries. Indian examples are often seen with elaborate soft-metal applied work, or damascening (*391*). Sometimes a dagger is screwed into the haft (*389*). See also *Biliong, Bullova*.

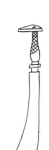

Ayda Katti   A short sword with heavy, wide curved single-edged blade, carried by the Coorgs of Malabar. The blade narrows at the hilt, which has no guard. The grip and large flat tear-shaped pommel are usually of wood with a chequered design, but sometimes examples are found with these parts in ivory. The weapon is carried on the back in circular brass holder with the blade exposed.

Bade-bade   A small Malayan knife with a slender, slightly curved, single-edged blade. The guardless hilt is usually of wood or horn. Its shape varies considerably but the commonest are of hoof or angled form (*363, 419*).

Bagh Nakh   An Indian 'tiger claw' weapon. The form is usually a bar with two loops, having four or five claw-like blades affixed at right angles (*415*).

Barong   An edged weapon with broad leaf-shaped blade about 16 inches in length, carried by the Moros of North Borneo and others in that area. The guardless hilt has an intricately carved angled pommel

84

usually with ornamental terminals. It may be of wood, horn or ivory, with a silver or brass ferrule (*420*).

Bhuj   An Indian hand weapon with broad heavy single-edged knife blade mounted in line with its haft. The blade is about 6 inches long and the haft, about 20 inches in length, often has a small knife which screws into the base. The bhuj is usually quite elaborate, being gold or silver damascened and sometimes having an elephant-head motif inset with semi-precious stones at the base of the blade.

Bichaq   A Turkish and Armenian dagger with straight single-edged blade, the hilt consisting of two plates of bone or ivory. It is often a small version of the yatagan (*q.v.*) and the sheath is frequently silver-mounted.

Bichwa   The Indian 'scorpion' dagger, with loop hilt and double-curved blade. Its form is taken from the earlier buffalo-horn daggers. Examples are sometimes seen with double forked blades (*406*), and they are occasionally combined with the bagh nakh.

Biliong   A Malayan axe, generally with a slender springy haft fashioned from a branch of a tree. It has a movable head and can be used as an adze with the blade at right angles to the haft.

Blowpipe   A long tube through which darts are blown. It is used in South America and some Eastern countries. The darts are often poisoned on the tip. See also *Sumpitan*.

Bolas   A South American Indian throwing weapon. It usually consists of three stone balls secured in leather covers which are joined by plaited leather cords. In use the bolas is spun round above the head until sufficient force is obtained for it to be released at speed. It is then aimed to entangle the legs of the animal to be caught.

Bolo   A Philippine short sword or long knife with fairly wide single-edged blade.

Boomerang   A throwing weapon generally of wood, with a flat surface and sharp edges. Some are slightly curved, others are quite angular. They are commonly Australian aboriginal weapons, but are used by some other native races.

Bow   The earliest and most widely used projectile weapon. In its simplest form it is a long strip of springy wood with a cord stretched between the two ends, the tension forming a slight arc. Composite bows of wood, horn and sinew were used by the Turks, Persians and other Eastern races. These usually appear of C shape when unstrung. See also *Yumi* (*under* Japanese Weapons).

Bullova   A war axe used by the wild tribesmen of Chota Nagpur, Central India. The haft is usually of plain wood and the iron heads vary in design from crescent shape to double-spiked.

Campilan   A Borneo sword with somewhat large hilt, the crosspiece of the same material as the grip and forked pommel. The latter is often decorated with hair tufts. The blade is single-edged and widens towards the tip.

Chakram   An Indian (Sikh) throwing ring or quoit. It is a flat steel ring with sharp outer edge and is made in varying sizes up to about 12 inches diameter.

Chilanum   An Indian all-steel dagger, with double-curved horn-shaped blade. The hilt is usually forged from the same piece of metal as the blade (*336*).

Club   Basically a stick with a heavy end, the club has been used from the earliest times to date. Numerous varieties are found from all parts of the world. Some have stone heads, others are finely carved (*421*). A rare variety is the club from the Marquesas Islands which has a large head carved with stylised human faces and geometrical designs (*354*).

Crossbow   Primitive forms of the crossbow were used by the Chinese and other Eastern peoples. They were usually made entirely of wood, but Chinese crossbow mechanisms in heavy bronze survive from ancient times. The Chinese had a repeating crossbow, *chu-ko-nu*, with box magazine fitted on top of the stock (*315*).

Damascening   The hammering of one metal on to another with a prepared surface to give a decorative effect. Gold and silver were much used in this manner on Indian weapons. The word is also used for the watered patterns on blades or barrels.

Dao   A sword used by the Nagas of Assam. The blade is virtually straight with cut-off tip. The plain wooden hilt has no guard. It is carried in an open-sided wooden scabbard with rattan binding and carrying loop.

Dha   The Burmese national sword. It has a single-edged blade with slight curvature. The hilt can be of wood, ivory (often carved) or silver, and it has no guard. The scabbard is of wood either bound with bands of rattan or mounted with silver, or even gold. They are often found with a thick red cord binding and loop for carrying. The dha varies in length from several inches to two or three feet (*398*).

Dhal   A circular shield used in India, Persia and other Asian countries. It is made of hide, brass or steel (often engraved and damascened) and usually has four domed bosses (*337*).

Executioner's Kris   A Malay kris with unusually long straight blade and generally straight hilt with rounded pommel. Executions were effected by plunging the blade down through the shoulder into the heart.

Fakir's Crutch   A short crutch used by Indian fakirs when seated. It served to support the body but was also, in fact, used as a weapon. The head was sometimes spiked and the haft frequently contained a concealed screw-in dagger.

Firangi   An Indian sword with long straight blade of European form. The blade was frequently fullered (grooved) and the hilt of khanda type (*q.v.*) had a spiked pommel.

Flyssa   A Moroccan sword or knife. The blade is single-edged and has a slender point. The guardless hilt is usually mounted with engraved brass, the wooden grips sometimes inlaid with brass and horn. The scabbards are of carved wood.

Golok   A Malayan jungle knife of machete type. The single-edged blade was heavy, with curved cutting edge and straight back. The weapon is found in varying sizes from knife to short sword.

Gupti   An Indian sword stick, usually fitted with a broad blade.

Hani   The New Zealand, Maori, staff of office. It is entirely of wood, sometimes elaborately carved overall, the base of spatulate form tapering to the head, which is of leaf shape. The head is carved with characteristic geometric whirls and has 'Tiki' masks inlaid with shell eyes.

Ishilunga   The oval cowhide shield carried by the Kaffir tribes of South Africa. It has a stick attached to the back and has two strips of hide interwoven at the centre to give strength.

I-wata-jinga   A stone-headed club used by the Plains Indians of North America. The haft was bound with hide, which also secured the head.

Ja-dagna   A wooden club used by the Plains Indians of North America. The head was carved as a ball, which sometimes had a spike attached (*392*).

Jambiya   An Arab dagger with curved blade. Many varieties are found from North Africa to India. The hilts are usually of horn, but

ivory and silver, or brass, is also often seen. The sheaths are frequently ornamental, the North African type having two large rings for suspension (*348, 350, 408–10, 414, 417*).

Kard   A Persian knife with straight single-edged blade, usually of fine Damascus steel. The guardless hilt was frequently of plain ivory.

Kaskara   A North African Arab sword with cruciform hilt. The straight double-edged blade is often European in form (*355*).

Kastane   The short sword from Ceylon. It had a curved blade, often European in origin. The hilt was of distinctive form decorated with monsters' heads and frequently embellished with silver or gold (*321*).

Katar   An Indian dagger designed for thrusting. It consists of tapered blade (the tip often reinforced for piercing chain mail) with a hilt formed of two parallel bars connected by two or more crossbars. Occasionally a knuckle guard is fitted (*326, 329*). Blades are found with 'scissors' action, serrated edges or are even forked (*327*).

Khanda   An Indian sword with broad spatulate blade. The back edge often had a strengthening band of ornamental steel. The hilt had a double-lobed guard with broad knuckle-bow and disc-shaped pommel. A curved spike continued from the pommel and this was used to obtain extra grip when the sword was used as a two-handed weapon (*345*). The khanda-type hilt is sometimes found on other Indian swords, e.g. firangi and tulwar; also on maces.

Khanjar   An Indo-Persian dagger, with slightly recurved blade often of finely patterned Damascus steel. The hilt, generally of 'pistol grip' shape, was usually of jade, carved or inset with gems (*418*).

Khanjarli   An Indian dagger with ribbed, double-curved blade. The hilt had a large flat crescent-shaped pommel usually of ivory.

Khyber Knife   The Afghan knife with straight-backed, tapered, single-edged blade and guardless hilt. The grips are of horn or ivory and when sheathed the hilt partly enters the mouth of the sheath. They are found in varying lengths from dagger to sword size (*330*).

Kilij   A Turkish sabre with broad-ended curved blade. The hilt has pistol-shaped horn or ivory grips, and a straight crosspiece with ball or pointed terminals. The scabbards are often silver or gilt mounted and have a hinged flap at the back to permit the blade to enter (*334, 339*).

Kindjal   A Caucasian knife generally with straight double-edged blade terminating in a sharp point. The blades are often fluted and bear makers' marks or inscriptions. The hilts have a semicircular or similarly shaped pommel, a narrow straight grip and are then wider where the blade adjoins. They are of horn or silver, sometimes embellished with niello work. The sheaths are leather covered, often with silver mounts or entirely of silver. Sometimes a small companion knife is found in the sheath (*338, 361*).

Klewang   A Malayan short sword with straight single-edged blade, widening slightly towards the tip. A variety of hilts and scabbards are found, often with silver mounts.

Knobkerrie   The South African, Kaffir, throwing stick or club. They are made of wood or rhino horn and have a large bulbous knob with slender haft, often tapering at the end. They are carved from one piece of wood or horn.

Kora   The Nepalese national sword. It has a heavy curved single-edged blade with pronounced widening at the end, which is engraved with a Buddhist symbol, often an eye (*423*).

Korambi   A small Sumatran knife with curved sickle-shaped blade. The horn hilts sometimes have a cut-out ring pommel.

Kotiate   A New Zealand, Maori, club. They are of wood or whalebone, double-lobed in form, and with carved pommel to the handle (*353*).

Kris   The widely used Malay dagger. Blades are finely watered and are found either straight or wavy in form. They widen at the top to a sharp point and the hilt fits straight on to the spiked tang, which continues from the top of the blade. The hilts of wood, ivory, etc., are often finely carved as the Garuda bird or demon figures (*349, 362, 366–9*). The kingfisher hilt is another, rare, type (*367*).

Kukri   The Gurkha knife, with heavy, single-edged blade, very sharp on the inner edge. There is a small semicircular depression near the hilt which is a phallic symbol having religious significance. The guardless hilt is usually of horn or ivory and sometimes of engraved steel or silver. The sheath is fitted with two small companion knives of similar shape, but may even have an assortment of accessories (*332, 412, 413*).

Lohar   A pick weapon used by an Indian Khyber tribe. The bill-shaped blade is at right angles to the decorated metal haft.

Macana   A South American, Guyanan, wooden club. It is rectangular in section with slender waisted middle and one broad end. Sometimes a polished stone is inserted in the head.

Mace   A club type of weapon, either all steel or with a steel head. The Persian mace often had a grotesque horned or bull's-head top. The Indian variety was flanged or had a spherical spiked head, the hilts being of khanda type (*396, 425, 426*).

Madu   An Indian combination thrusting and parrying weapon. It consists of a small circular shield with a pair of steel-tipped buck horns attached to the back and pointing out in opposite directions.

Mandau   A Dyak headhunter's sword. The blade is almost straight and is single-edged. The angled hilt is of carved staghorn or wood, decorated with tufts of hair. The scabbard is also carved, bound with cane and ornamented with tufts of hair (*424*).

Mere   A New Zealand, Maori, club, made of green stone. It is plain, spatulate in form and with polished surface.

Moro Kris   A distinctive form of kris used by the Moros of Mindanao, Philippine Islands. It is larger than usual, with broad double-edged wavy blade of even width. The hilt often has an elaborately carved wood or ivory pommel of recurved form, similar to a barong (*q.v.*).

Nimcha   A Moroccan sabre. The hilt has a broad grip with angled pommel, a right-angled knuckle-bow and down-drooping quillons (*341*).

Nzappa Zap   A Congo axe. The openwork iron head has twisted sections and is often decorated with human faces. The haft is covered with copper or snakeskin. These were sometimes used as a form of currency.

Parang   A Malayan jungle knife or machete; various forms are seen.

Pata   An Indian gauntlet sword. The usual form has a straight blade, often of European origin, and a steel or brass gauntlet hilt derived from the katar (*q.v.*) which covers the hand and forearm. It could only be used as a thrusting weapon, probably by horsemen.

Pattisa   An Indian sword with broad spatulate blade, widening towards the tip which is rounded. The hilt is similar to that of a khanda (*q.v.*).

Patu   The New Zealand, Maori, war club of bone, wood or stone. It is polished, spatulate in form and has sharp edges.

Pesh-kabz   An Indo-Persian dagger with slender pointed blade of T section. The heavy guardless hilt often has ivory grips.

Phurbu   A Tibetan ceremonial dagger used by the Lamas for exorcising evil spirits. It is usually entirely of brass, the hilt of thunderbolt form and with grotesque masks (*399, 407*).

Pichangatti   A Coorg knife with short, wide, heavy single-edged blade. The guardless hilt has a slender grip with large round pommel. The sheath and hilt are frequently mounted and embellished with silver or brass. A chain is attached to the sheath, from which tweezers and other implements are suspended.

Piha-kaetta   A dagger from Ceylon. The blades are single-edged and vary in width. The hilts have no guard and are mounted on the blade with an elaborate silver or brass plate. The grips of wood, ivory, etc., are intricately carved and have silver or brass pommels (*333*).

Pulouar   An Indian sword of tulwar type, with curved blade. The hilt has down-drooping quillons and no knuckle-bow.

Qama   The national weapon of Georgia, similar in form to the kindjal (*q.v.*). The hilts and sheaths are often of silver inset with coral.

Ram Dao   A Nepalese sacrificial sword with heavy broad blade. The end is curved and bears an inlaid or engraved eye symbol. The hilt continues straight in line from the back edge of the blade (*380*).

Saif   An Arab sabre. The hilt has a pistol-shaped grip with a boss on the pommel (*319*).

Seme   The East African, Masai, sword. The blade is double-edged and widens towards the tip. The hilt has a small grip bound with hide and no guard. The scabbard is covered with hide.

Shamshir   A Persian sabre with curved blade of even width. The hilt generally has a straight crosspiece of steel or silver-gilt, and ivory grips with right-angled pommel (*317, 318*).

Shashqa   A Caucasian sabre with broad single-edged grooved blade. The guardless hilt is of pistol-grip shape with pommel divided into two wings. The hilt and scabbard are often mounted with niello silver work (*324*).

Shotel   The national sword of Abyssinia, with much-curved double-edged blade. The guardless hilt is of wood.

Spear   A long pointed weapon used for thrusting, or throwing. It is used by many races and various forms are found. The heads are usually of iron, but stone, horn and other materials have been used.

Spear Thrower   An implement used to assist in the throwing of a spear. Most forms are of wood, flat in form and with a hooked end.

Sumpitan   The Dyak blowpipe (*q.v.*).

Tamarang   An Australian Aboriginal parrying shield, carved from the solid, and with incised geometrical decoration.

Telek   The Tuareg arm dagger. It has a cruciform hilt, often of brass. The sheath has a loop which is placed over the wrist (*328*).

Tewha-tewha   A Maori wooden club with pointed haft and hatchet-shaped head, carved from the solid.

Toki   A Maori axe. Some were fitted with European iron-trade heads, and these were used for fighting. Others had stone heads. The hafts were of wood or, sometimes, carved bone.

Tomahawk   The North American Indian fighting axe. Early forms had a stone head and later types an iron head. The latter were traded by the whites and often had a pipe bowl on the back (*394*).

Trident   A triple-bladed spear. Examples are found from Persia, India, Java and China. The latter, with widely spaced blades, was used to fight the tiger.

Tulwar   The Indian curved sword. The hilt usually has a knuckle-bow and has a disc pommel, and is frequently damascened. The blade is single-edged and often of finely watered steel (*381*).

Wahaika   A short Maori club with curved blade. It is made of wood or bone and frequently carved (*351*).

Yatagan   A Turkish sword with slightly recurved single-edged blade. The guardless hilt has grips of ivory, horn, silver, etc., often with large-eared pommel (*320, 322, 323*).

Zaghnal   An Indian axe with right-angled bill-shaped blade.

Japanese Weapons

Aikuchi   A dagger without a guard (tsuba). These were carried by retired warriors as an indication that, although they no longer sought trouble, they would still defend themselves. When mounted in plain whitewood hilts and sheaths they could be used for ceremonial suicide (*335, 374*).

Cloisonné Enamel   A finish sometimes used on highly decorative Japanese swords and daggers. It was formed by a series of soft-metal wires or ribbons, soldered to a metal ground, with coloured enamels applied within the panels formed by the wires or ribbons.

Daisho ('great and little')   The two Japanese swords, katana and wakizashi (*q.v.*), worn by the samurai. The mounts and scabbards are usually of the same design.

Fuchi   The mount at the base of the hilt next to the tsuba. It is usually made as a pair to the kashira (*q.v.*) or pommel cap, in the same metal and with matching or complementary design (*404*).

Habaki   The metal ferrule fitted round the sword blade just below the tsuba. It serves to hold the blade firmly in the scabbard, also acting as a washer to keep out the atmosphere when the sword is sheathed.

Hachiwara   A helmet breaker, consisting of an iron bar of rectangular section, slightly curved and with a small hook near the hilt. It had a sheath similar to that of a dagger. Another use for this implement is considered to be as a sword breaker.

Hamidashi   A dagger with a small tsuba only slightly larger in diameter than the grip. The tsuba has only shallow concave indentations on the sides, against which the kodzuka and kogai rest, as opposed to the oval holes on the tanto tsuba, through which they pass.

90

Hayago   A Japanese powder flask. They are mostly made of lacquered wood, papier-mâché or horn.

Horimono   The chiselled design on a blade in form of a dragon, thunderbolt or other design.

Jin Tachi   A heavy long double-handed sword.

Jitte   A short club or baton in the form of a rod with side hook at the base of the handle. They were used as a parrying weapon and sometimes carried by police.

Kakihan   A craftsman's personal mark often found on sword mounts, etc., usually below the signature.

Kashira   The pommel-cap mount of a sword or dagger, usually decorated *en suite* with the fuchi (*q.v.*) (*404*).

Katana   A fighting sword with blade approximately 27 inches in length. One of the most common types found. Its use continued through the Second World War, when it was usually fitted in standard military mounts. It was carried by the samurai edge upwards, pushed through the girdle (*376*). See also *Daisho*.

Katana Kake   A sword-stand. It is usually lacquered and has upright end pieces with two or more U-shaped notches, on which all swords, except tachi, were laid horizontally, blades edge uppermost. Another variety was for the tachi, on which the sword was placed vertically, point upwards.

Katana Zutsu   A sword-case, usually of lacquered wood, cylindrical in shape and made in two sections. The centre swells out to take the tsuba (*375*).

Ken   An ancient type of sword with straight double-edged blade, only surviving as a ceremonial temple sword (*347, 377*).

Kodzuka   The small knife often found fitted in a slot on the side of the sword scabbard or dagger sheath. The handle is also known by the same name, and is usually ornamental. The blade is frequently inscribed (*404*).

Kogai   A skewer-like implement sometimes found in a slot in the side of a sword scabbard or dagger sheath. Its exact use is not certain but it is variously thought to have been a hair-arranging pin, an identification mark left in the head of a dead enemy, or a means of securing the sword in the scabbard. Sometimes it is made in two sections (wori-kogai), possibly for use as chopsticks.

Koi-guchi   The mouth of the scabbard, frequently of horn.

Kojiri   The end mount or chape of a scabbard or sheath.

Koto   An 'old' blade, made between A.D. 900 and 1530.

Kurikata   A looped mount on the side of the scabbard or sheath through which the sageo (*q.v.*) cord is passed.

Kwaiken   A small ladies' dagger of simple form, sometimes used for ceremonial suicide.

Mekugi   The bamboo peg which secured the hilt to the tang of the blade.

Mekugi Ana   The mounting hole in the tang of the blade through which the hilt is secured by the mekugi (*q.v.*).

Menuki   Small ornaments, usually a pair, fitted beneath the cord binding of the hilt. These were originally intended to hold the mekugi (*q.v.*) secure, but are not now found in that position. They do, however, help to improve the hand grip on the hilt.

Mokko   A common form of tsuba in the shape of four lobes.

AW—G

Naginata   The spear with long, curved sword-like blade. The haft is usually lacquered and fitted with metal mounts and the blade has a lacquer sheath.

Nakago   The tang of a blade. They are frequently signed and may have more than one mounting hole (mekugi ana).

Namban   A style of decoration frequently seen on sword fittings. Usually of iron, in most cases they have complex openwork and chiselled designs of dragons and scrolls.

Nanako   A ground of minute raised dots, made with a cupped punch, giving a 'fish roe' appearance.

Nashiji   A style of lacquer used on scabbards, having a flecked gold or mother-of-pearl appearance.

Origane   A small hook, sometimes found on the scabbard, to prevent it from sliding through the girdle. It is alternatively known as the sakatsuno.

Sageo   The flat silk braid found on the scabbard or sheath. It passes through the kurikata (*q.v.*).

Same   Skin of the giant ray used for hilt covering and scabbard decoration, the latter often polished smooth and lacquered, the nodules of the same showing through lacquer, giving the effect of a scatter of stars.

Saya   The scabbard of a Japanese sword. It is made of two halves of wood internally carved to fit the blade. The saya is of oval section and usually lacquered.

Sentoku   A yellow bronze alloy consisting of copper, tin and zinc.

Seppa   The oval washers fitted on each side of the tsuba.

Shakudo   An alloy of copper with about 3–6% of gold, much used in Japanese sword furniture, purple-blue in colour. It formed an excellent ground for the inlay of gold, silver or copper.

Shibuichi   An alloy of copper and silver, the latter about 25%, used in Japanese sword furniture giving shades of grey. The proportions varied to as much as 50% of each metal.

Shinto   'New' blades, made after 1530, as opposed to koto (*q.v.*).

Shirasaya   The plain wooden scabbard and hilt in which fine blades are stored. They are frequently inscribed with details of the blade.

Signatures   The tangs of sword blades often bear a signature and this is of help in identification, although sometimes they are false. The tsuba, kodzuka, kogai and fuchi kashira may also bear signatures.

Sode Garami   A polearm with barbed and spiked head. Used as a sleeve-tangler to catch villains.

Soritsuno   The small hook sometimes found on the side of a sheath, serving to retain it in the belt as the dagger is drawn. Also known as origane.

Tachi   A court sword, distinguished by the scabbard mounting which has two slings for suspension from the belt. The mounts of a tachi have a different set of names to those of other swords (*365*).

Tanto   A dagger fitted with a tsuba, as opposed to the aikuchi (*q.v.*) which has no guard (*371, 373*).

Teppo   Japanese firearms. Both pistols and guns were made, the majority with matchlock ignition. The barrels were frequently signed and often finely inlaid with silver (*141*).

Tsuba   The guard of a sword or tanto. It is the most important and valuable item of sword furniture (*402, 403*).

Tsuchi   The small hammer used to remove the mekugi (*q.v.*) in order to dismount the hilt.

Tsuka   The hilt of a sword or dagger. It is made of two halves of wood, cut to the shape of the tang, and usually covered with ray skin (same). It is then bound with braid and mounted with fuchi kashira and menuki (*q.v.*).

Uchiwa   One form of war fan, comprising a handle with two flat side wings. It did not fold..

Uchihimo   The braid binding on the hilt of a sword or dagger, which also serves to secure the kashira (*q.v.*) in place.

Umebari   A sharp-pointed instrument sometimes found in place of the kogai. It was used for a type of acupuncture to liven up torpid horses, usually by the people of Higo.

Wakizashi   A short sword with blade about 18 inches long. Often the companion sword to the katana, also worn edge upwards through the girdle. The scabbard of the wakizashi frequently had a slot to contain the kodzuka, and often also one for the kogai (*370*).

War Fan   A folding fan of strong lacquered paper with iron side pieces, used as a club or parrying weapon. See also uchiwa for another type.

Ya   An arrow. They are long and often have fine heads yano-ne (*q.v.*).

Yakiba   The pattern, often with a wavy boundary, seen near the cutting edge of a blade, and formed by the metals composing it.

Yano-ne   An arrowhead. Various types are found, some with pierced designs. A bifurcated type was used for cutting the rigging of ships. The tangs are often signed.

Yari   A spear with straight double-edged blade, sometimes having one or two right-angled blades at the base (*405*).

Yoroi Toshi   An armour-piercing dagger.

Yumi   The Japanese bow. It is composed of strips of bamboo and wood, secured by fish glue, lacquered over and bound at intervals with rattan. It is about 6 feet 5 inches in length. See also Ya (arrow).

317 A Persian sabre, shamshir. Blade 30″.

318 A Persian sabre, shamshir. Blade 33″.

319 An Arab sabre, saif. Blade 29½″.

320 A Turkish yataghan. Blade 26″.

321 A Ceylon sword, kastane. Blade 19″.

322 A Turkish yataghan with walrus ivory-eared hilt. Blade 24″.

323 A Turkish yataghan with silver-eared hilt. Blade 21″.

324 A Cossack sabre, shashqa, with nielloed silver hilt. Blade 30″.

325 A Burmese dha dagger. Blade 6½″.

326 An Indian katar, with knuckle guard cast as a monster head. Blade 14″.

Eastern and native swords and daggers.

327 A scissors katar. Blade 8″.

328 A Tuareg arm dagger, telek. Blade 10″.

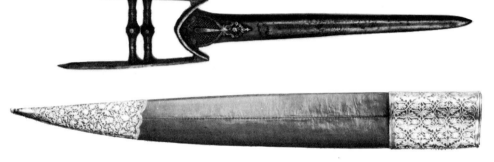

329 A katar. Blade 14½″.

330 A Khyber knife, with silver-mounted sheath. Blade 19″.

331 A Balkan flintlock pistol with all-metal stock, the rat-tail butt with 'key' end. 22″ overall, barrel 11″.

332 A Gurkha kukri in silver-mounted sheath. Blade 11″.

333 A Ceylon dagger, piha-kaetta, with sheath. Blade 8″.

Eastern weapons.

334 A Turkish sabre, kilij. Blade 32″.

335 (extreme left) A Japanese dagger, aikuchi. Blade 13″.

336 (left) An Indian dagger, chilanum. Blade 12″.

337 (centre) An Indo-Persian shield, dhal. Diameter 21″.

338 (right) Two Caucasian daggers, kindjal. Blades 13½″.

339 A Turkish sabre, kilij. Blade 32″.

340 An Indian tulwar with monster-head hilt. Blade 30″.

341 A Moroccan sabre, nimcha, in its scabbard. Blade 28½″.

AW—G*

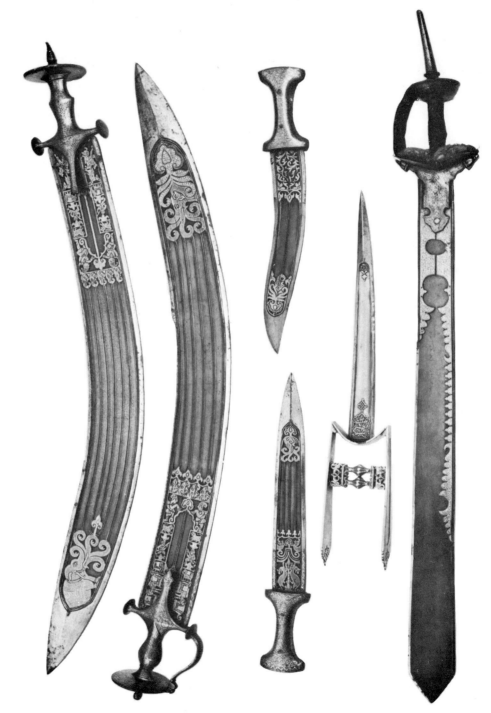

342 (left) Two Indian executioners' swords. Blades 30″ × 3″ wide.

343 (centre) Two Indian all-steel daggers. Blades 11″ and 12″.

344 (right) An Indian dagger, katar. Blade 13½″.

345 (extreme right) An Indian sword, khanda. Blade 28″.

Indian and other swords and daggers.

346 A Luristan bronze sword. 18″ overall.

347 A Japanese ken dagger. Blade 9″.

348 A Persian jambiya with jade hilt. Blade 10″.

349 A Malay kris with flamboyant blade. 14¼″.

350 A small Persian jambiya. Blade 6″.

351 A New Zealand club, wahaika. 14½″.

352 A Luristan bronze axe-head. 8″ overall.

353 A New Zealand club, kotate.

Daggers and native weapons.

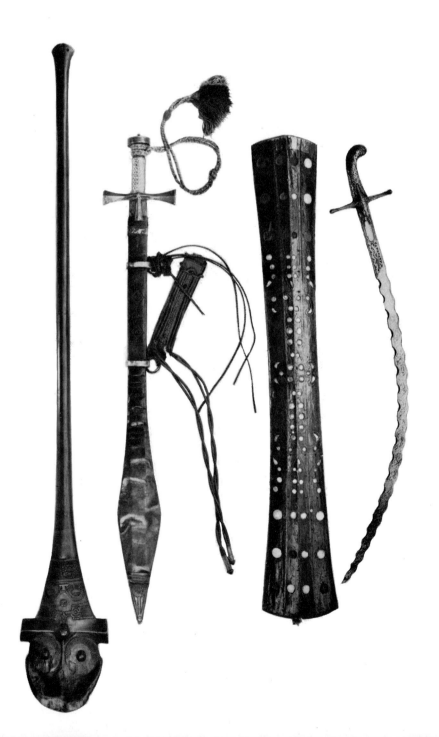

354 (extreme left) A carved wood club from the Marquesas Islands. 58″ overall.

355 (left) A Sudanese sword, kaskara. Blade 35″.

356 (right) An Indonesian shield. 41½″.

357 (extreme right) A Persian shamshir with flamboyant blade. 33½″.

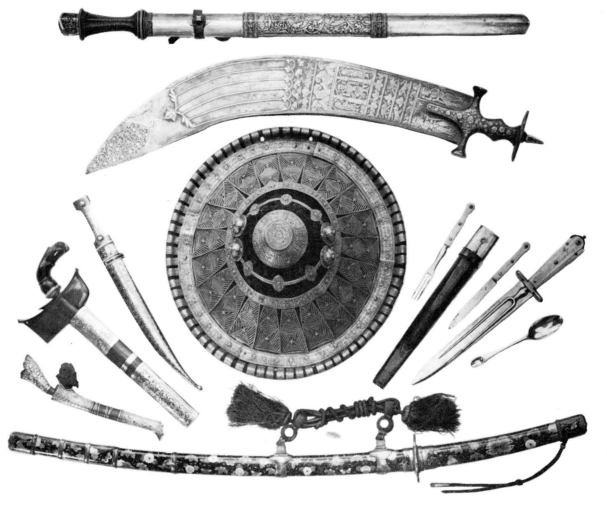

358 A Tibetan sword. Blade 26½″.

359 An Indian executioner's sword. Blade 29″×4¼″ wide.

360 (centre) An Abyssinian shield. Diameter 17½″.

361 (top) A Caucasian kindjal. Blade 12″.

362 (centre) A Malay kris. Blade 12″.

363 (bottom) A Malay bade-bade. Blade 7″.

364 A Continental hunting trousse, five pieces. Knife blade 11″.

365 A Japanese sword, tachi, the hilt and scabbard entirely of cloisonné enamel. Blade 27″.

Oriental and other swords and daggers.

366   A Malay kris with gold inlaid blade, 13¾″.

367 (centre)   A Malay kris with kingfisher hilt. Blade 13½″.

368   A Malay kris with ivory hilt. Blade 13″.

369   A Malay kris with carved bone hilt. Blade 14″.

Malay kris.

370 A Japanese short
sword, wakizashi. Blade
$16\frac{1}{2}''$.

371 A Japanese dagger,
tanto. Blade 13″.

372 A Japanese World
War II naval dirk. Blade $8\frac{3}{4}''$.

373 A Japanese dagger,
tanto. Blade 10″.

374 A Japanese dagger,
aikuchi. Blade $8\frac{3}{4}''$.

375 A Japanese sword-case,
katana zutsu.

376 A Japanese sword,
katana, the tsuba dis-
mounted. Blade $26\frac{1}{2}''$.

377 A Japanese ken-type
sword with dragon horimono
on $27\frac{1}{2}''$ blade.

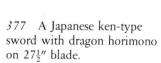

Japanese daggers and swords.

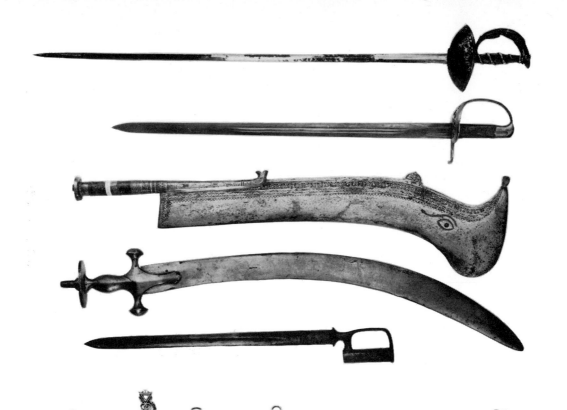

378 A French exhibition rapier. Blade 36½″. Mid-nineteenth century.

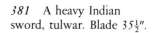

379 A sword bayonet for the Jacob's double-barrelled rifle. Blade 30″.

380 A Nepalese sacrificial axe, ram dao. Blade 31″.

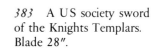

381 A heavy Indian sword, tulwar. Blade 35½″.

382 An all-steel pattern 1845 sapper's and miner's sword bayonet. Blade 22½″.

383 A US society sword of the Knights Templars. Blade 28″.

384 A Zanzibar sword with silver mounts. Blade 30½″.

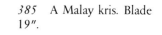

385 A Malay kris. Blade 19″.

386 A Japanese carved ivory sword. Blade 19″.

387 An Arab sabre in silver-mounted scabbard. Blade 28½″.

388 An English silver-hilted small-sword. Blade 30″. Mid-eighteenth century.

389 An Indian axe, 18″, with crescent-shaped head, the engraved copper-gilt haft with screw-in dagger (blade 7″).

390 An Indian elephant goad, ancus. 23″.

391 An Indian all-steel axe, 30″, with engraved crescent-shaped head.

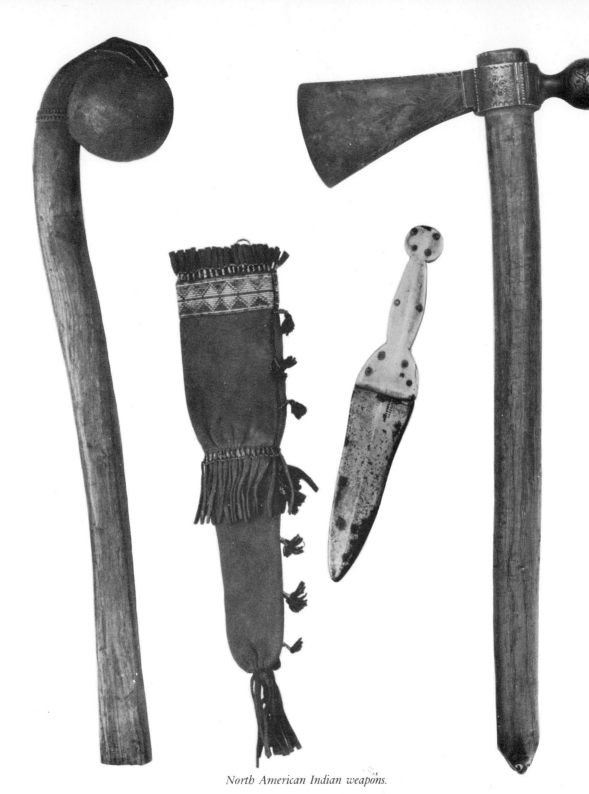

392 A North American Plains Indian club, ja dagna. 24".

393 Red Indian beaver-tail knife with buckskin sheath. Blade 7".

394 A Red Indian tomahawk pipe. 14½".

North American Indian weapons.

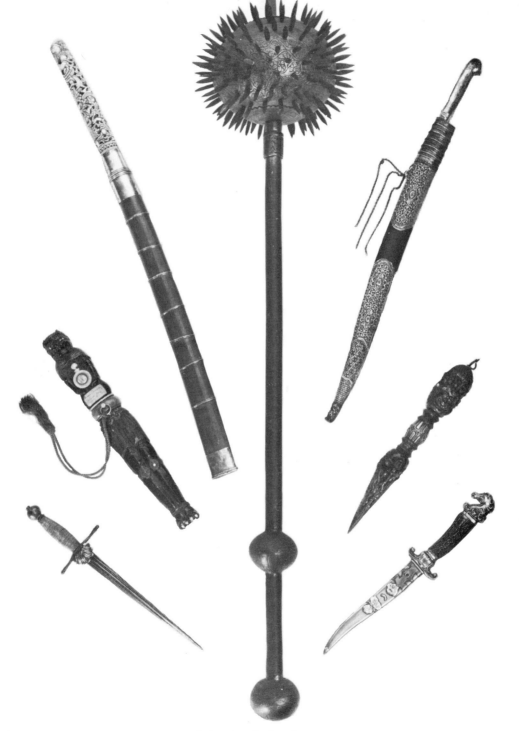

396 An Indian all-steel
spiked mace. 38".

398 A Burmese dha with
carved ivory hilt. Blade 20".

397 A Turkish yatagan.
Blade 20½".

395 A Japanese ken dagger,
the hilt and sheath of demon
form. Blade 8½".

399 A Tibetan phurbu.
15" overall.

400 A German left-hand
dagger. Blade 10½". Early
seventeenth century.

401 A Victorian Bowie
knife with horse-head
pommel. Blade 7½".

Oriental and other daggers.

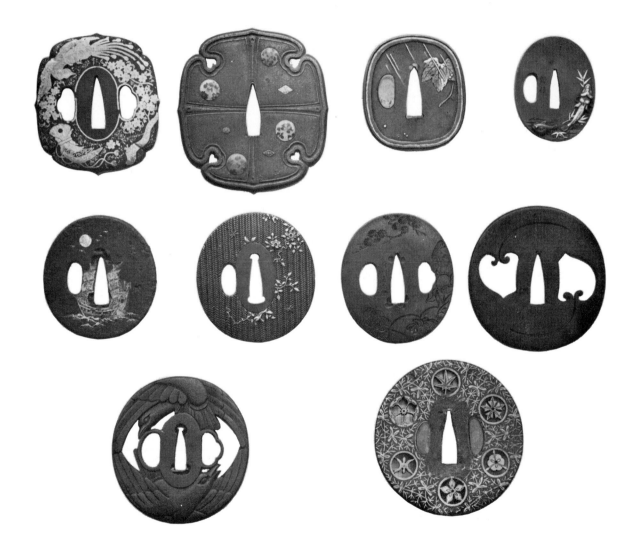

402   A group of Japanese sword guards, tsuba.

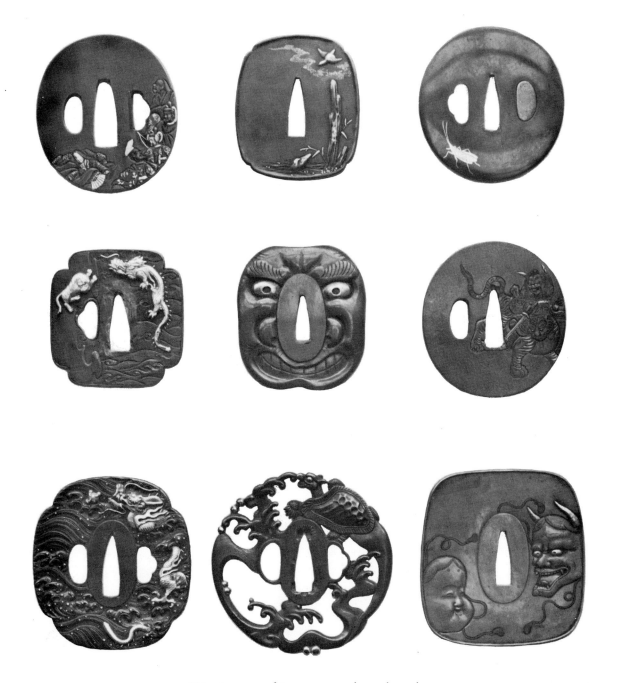

403   A group of Japanese sword guards, tsuba.

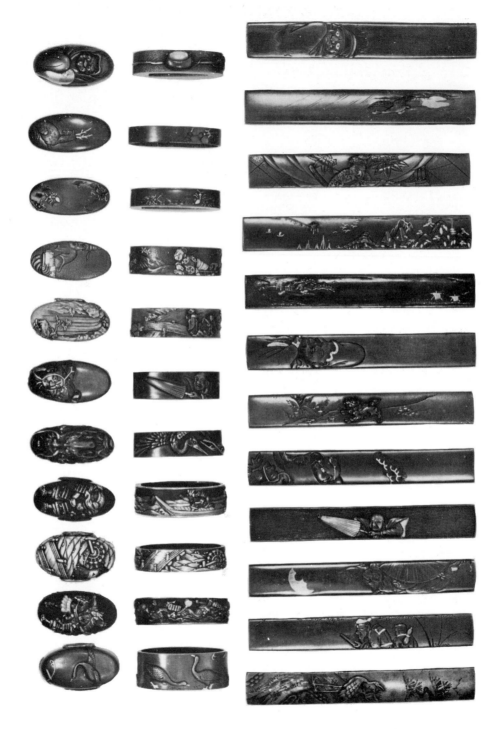

404 A group of Japanese sword mounts: kodzuka, fuchi and kashira.

405 A display of Japanese polearm heads, yari; (*in the centre*) an Indo-Persian shield, dhal.

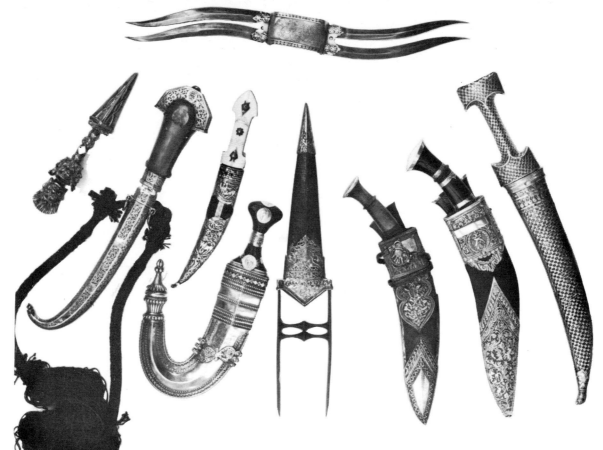

406 An Indian double-ended dagger, bichwa. 20½", blades 7½".

Left-hand group

407 *(left)* A Tibetan phurbu. Blade 4".

408 *(centre)* A Moroccan jambiya. Blade 9½".

409 *(right)* An Arabian jambiya. Blade 6¾".

410 *(below, right)* A southern Indian jambiya, in U-shaped silver sheath. Blade 8".

411 *(centre)* An Indian dagger, katar. Blade 10".

412 *(left)* A kukri. Blade 10½".

413 *(centre)* A kukri. Blade 12½".

414 *(right)* An Albanian jambiya, the hilt and sheath of silver.

415 Three Indian tiger's-claw weapons, bagh nakh. Average length 7".

110   *Indian and other daggers.*

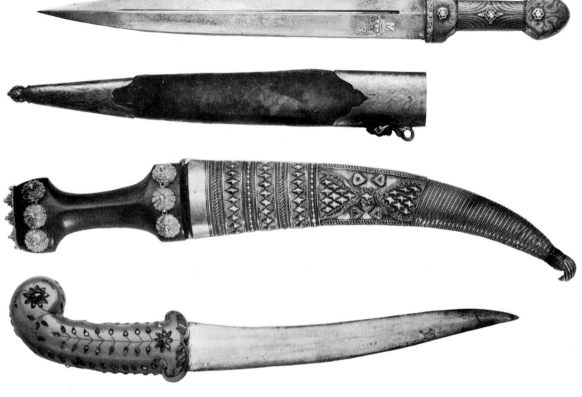

416 A Caucasian dagger, kindjal, with sheath. Blade 14½″.

417 A Balkan jambiya. Blade 8½″. .

418 An Indian dagger, khanjar, with inlaid jade hilt. Blade 10½″.

419 A Malayan knife, bade-bade, in silver-covered sheath. Blade 8¾″.

420 A barong, with carved ivory pommel. Blade 18″.

Indian and Malay daggers.

421 An African wooden club with carved head.

422 A sword from Malabar with sickle-ended blade. 27″.

423 A Nepalese sword, kora. Blade 22″.

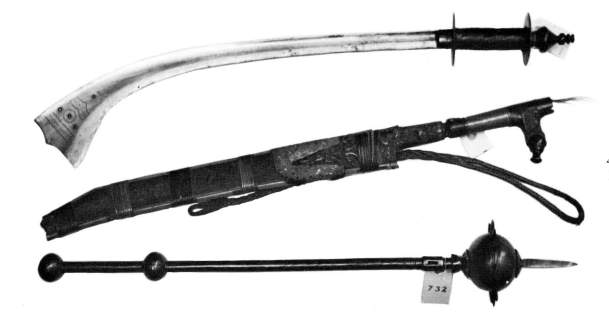

424 A Borneo head-hunter's sword. Blade 23½″.

425 An Indian all-steel mace with spiked head. 30″ overall.

426 A Persian all-steel mace with demon head. 36″.

Indian and native swords and maces.

Bibliography

ABELS, ROBERT   *Bowie Knives*   New York

ATKINSON, JOHN A.   *Duelling Pistols*   London, 1964

AYLWARD, J. D.   *The Small-sword in England*   New revised edition, London, 1960

BAXTER, D. R.   *Superimposed Load Firearms 1360–1860*   Hong Kong, 1966

BLACKMORE, HOWARD L.   *Arms and Armour*   London, 1965

BLACKMORE, HOWARD L.   *British Military Firearms 1650–1850*   London, 1961

BLACKMORE, HOWARD L.   *Firearms*   London, 1964

BLACKMORE, HOWARD L.   *Guns and Rifles of the World*   London, 1965

BLAIR, CLAUDE   *European and American Arms c. 1100–1850*   London, 1962

BLANCH, H. J.   *A Century of Guns*   London, 1909

BOSANQUET, CAPT. HENRY T. A., CVO, RN, FSA   *The Naval Officer's Sword*   HMSO, London, 1955

BOWMAN, HANK W.   *Antique Guns*   USA, 1953

CAREY, A. MERWIN   *English, Irish and Scottish Firearms Makers*   London, 1954

CHAPEL, C. E.   *The Gun Collector's Handbook of Values*   Third revised edition, New York, 1955

CHAPEL, C. E.   *US Martial and Semi-martial Single-shot Pistols*   New York, 1962

DOWELL, W. C.   *The Webley Story*   Leeds, 1962

DUNLAP, JACK   *American, British and Continental Pepperbox Firearms*   California, 1964

EGERTON, LORD, OF TATTON   *Indian and Oriental Armour*   New edition, London, 1968

FFOULKES, CHARLES   *Arms and Armament: An Historical Survey of the Weapons of the British Army*   London, 1945

FFOULKES, CHARLES and HOPKINSON, E. C.   *Sword, Lance and Bayonet*   Second edition, London, 1967

GEORGE, J. N.   *English Guns and Rifles*   USA, 1947

GEORGE, J. N.   *English Pistols and Revolvers*   USA, 1938

GERMAN, MICHAEL C.   *A Guide to Oriental Daggers and Swords*   London, 1967

GLENDENNING, IAN   *British Pistols and Guns 1640–1840*   Second edition, London, 1967

HAYWARD, JOHN F.   *The Art of the Gunmaker 1500–1830*   2 vols., London, 1962/3

JACKSON, H. J.   *European Hand Firearms of the Sixteenth, Seventeenth and Eighteenth Centuries* (with *Treatise on Scottish Hand Firearms* by C. E. WHITELAW)   Second edition, London, 1959

LATHAM, JOHN W.   *British Military Swords: From 1800 to the Present Day*   London, 1966

LATHAM, R. J. WILKINSON   *British Military Bayonets 1700–1945*   London, 1967

LENK, TORSTEN   *The Flintlock: Its Origin and Development*   London edition, 1965

MANN, SIR JAMES, KCVO   *Wallace Collection Catalogue of European Arms and Armour* (Volume I, *Armour*, and Volume II, *Arms*)   London, 1962

MAY, COMMANDER W. E., RN and KENNARD, A. N., FSA   *Naval Swords and Firearms*   Booklet, HMSO, 1962

NEAL, W. KEITH   *Spanish Guns and Pistols*   London, 1955

NEAL, W. KEITH and BACK, D. H. L.   *The Mantons: Gunmakers*   London, 1967

NEWMAN, ALEX R. and RYERSON, E.　*Japanese Art: A Collector's Guide*　London, 1964

NORMAN, VESEY　*Arms and Armour*　London, 1964

OAKESHOTT, R. EWART　*The Archaeology of Weapons*　London, 1960

OAKESHOTT, R. EWART　*The Sword in the Age of Chivalry*　London, 1964

PENROSE, E. H.　*Descriptive Catalogue of the Collection of Firearms in the Museum of Applied Science of Victoria*　Victoria, Australia, 1949

PETERSON, HAROLD L.　*American Knives*　New York, 1958

PETERSON, H. L.　*Encyclopaedia of Firearms*　USA, 1967

POLLARD, MAJOR H. B. C.　*A History of Firearms*　London, 1926

RICKETTS, HOWARD　*Firearms*　London, 1962

RILING, RAY　*The Powder Flask Book*　Pennsylvania, USA, 1953

ROADS, C. H.　*The British Soldier's Firearm 1850–1864*　London, 1964

ROBINSON, B. W.　*The Arts of the Japanese Sword*　London, 1961

SERVEN, JAMES E.　*Colt Firearms 1836–1954*　California, 1954

SMITH, W. H. B.　*Gas, Air and Spring Guns of the World*　Pennsylvania, USA, 1957

STEPHENS, F. J.　*Bayonets: An Illustrated History and Reference Guide*　London, 1968

STONE, GEORGE CAMERON　*A Glossary of the Construction, Decoration and Use of Arms and Armour, in All Countries and in All Times*　Portland, Maine, 1934

TAYLERSON, A. W. F.　*The Revolver 1865–1888*　London, 1966

TAYLERSON, A. W. F.　*Revolving Arms*　London, 1967

TAYLERSON, A. W. F., ANDREWS, R. A. N. and FRITH, J.　*The Revolver 1818–1865*　London, 1968

VALENTINE, ERIC　*Rapiers*　London, 1968

WENHAM, EDWARD　*Antiques A–Z*　Twelfth edition, London, 1967

WILKINSON, FREDERICK　*Small Arms*　London, 1965

WILKINSON, FREDERICK　*Swords and Daggers*　London, 1967

WINANT, LEWIS　*Early Percussion Firearms*　New York, 1959

WINANT, LEWIS　*Firearms Curiosa*　New York, 1961

WINANT, LEWIS　*Pepperbox Firearms*　New York, 1952